To Ric
With love
from Joan
Xmas '79

HURRICANE HAZEL

HURRICANE HAZEL

Betty Kennedy

Macmillan of Canada
Toronto

Canadian Cataloguing in Publication Data

Kennedy, Betty, 1926–
Hurricane Hazel

ISBN 0-7705-1821-4

1. Ontario – Hurricane, 1954. I. Title.

QC959.C3K46   551.5'52'09713   C79-094568-1

Printed in Canada for
The Macmillan Company of Canada Limited
70 Bond Street
Toronto, Ontario
M5B 1X3

Contents

Preface

Since I lived for more than sixteen years on a ravine overlooking the Humber River and witnessed the metamorphosis of that valley from a flood-savaged landscape to an idyllic parkland, Hurricane Hazel had more than a passing fascination for me. The hurricane story is one that needs no embellishment. Ordinary people caught up in extraordinary circumstances do courageous, poignant, incredible things. Perhaps most remarkable of all, they willingly and generously share those experiences with others as they have in this book.

When people heard about the book through CFRB, CBC's Front Page Challenge, and the *Toronto Daily Star,* letters came pouring in from every province in Canada. People wrote, granted interviews, and engaged in long conversations on the phone, telling of their personal experiences. You will meet many of them in these pages and often hear their stories in their own words, for there is a quality of realism to what many have to say that cannot be matched by another's storytelling.

For a time it puzzled me that so many individuals who had personally met disaster should be able to go back and relive it. Gradually I came to feel that in a curious and complex way their retelling did many things: it was at once a way of saying, "Yes, I remember," and "We have been able to survive." And it was also a way of expressing a never-ending wonderment at the life force that is in us all. The remembering is a reaffirmation of life.

I am more grateful than I know how to say to all of those who came forward with their stories. I regret only that the physical dimensions of a book made a limited choice of these accounts necessary.

I am grateful also to Doug Gibson for his skilled and sensitive advice and editing; to Mark Kennedy for research; to Ruth Carlisle for manuscript-typing; and to my dear family for their infinite patience and encouragement.

Betty Kennedy
Toronto: May 1979

To all those
whose lives were touched by Hurricane Hazel

HURRICANE HAZEL

CHAPTER ONE

"HURACÁN"

Hurricane. The very word seems to carry some of its meaning in its sound. You can almost hear the howl of winds in the beginning of the word, while the hard cracking sound of the last syllable gives the sense of things breaking before its force. It's a word that rings in the ears and evokes immediate mental images of raging seas; of palms that rattle and are bent as if they were grass; and of sand and rain that become like arrows driven by the fury of the wind.

But to most Canadians a hurricane belongs to other people, other places. Hurricanes are part of that technicolour world of movies or television – of larger-than-life, wide-screen, man-against-the-elements epics set in the lush world of the tropics. Real enough, but having little to do with our world.

When we see newspaper or television coverage of a hurricane (often photographed prudently from the air) showing its carnage and devastation, we may pause for a moment and wonder what it must feel like to be caught in one. What must it be like to have rooftops blow off above you and walls collapse around you, to see trees, animals, and even cars sent hurtling through the air by the shrieking wind? We can feel a quick sympathy for the poor victims left drenched, numbed, homeless, and bereaved by the storm. But there is still an air of unreality about it . . . like a war movie to someone who has never been part of a war. Those things happen somewhere else, in remote, exotic places. To Canadians, hurricanes are only of academic interest.

The exact origins of hurricanes are still unclear, but scientists tell us they are born only in tropical regions and develop only over water warmer than 81 degrees Fahrenheit. Any wind of force twelve (the highest possible range on the Beaufort Scale) with a velocity over seventy-three miles per hour qualifies as a hurricane. But over time the word has come to mean a cyclone that occurs in the West Indies and the Gulf of Mexico, while the equivalent in the Pacific is known as a "typhoon" – appropriately enough, "great wind" in Chinese. The hurricane season runs from May to December, with the most frequent occurrences in September and October.

In its early stages a hurricane moves in a generally westerly direction in the trade-wind belts, gradually curving to the right as it enters temperate latitudes. Its diameter ranges from twenty-five to six hundred miles; when well developed it is accompanied by very heavy rainfall, astonishingly low barometric pressure (often less than 28.5 inches at the centre), and winds that can range from seventy-five to two hundred miles per hour.

Fully developed, the hurricane is the most destructive of all storms, because of its size and savage intensity. Tornadoes – as Canadians on the Prairies know only too well – can generate a terrifying wind force. (In 1953 a freak tornado in Sarnia left bicycles from the street hanging from the outside of a building five storeys up.) But, as a Manitoban in Allan Anderson's book *Remembering the Farm* reveals, the tornado's funnel can be so narrow that it can pick up a combine on one side of a yard and crush it to scrap, while leaving bales of hay a few yards away completely untouched. In almost every case, a tornado's path is less than a quarter of a mile in width. By contrast, the winds of a hurricane frequently blanket thousands of square miles. Measuring the actual velocity of hurricane-force winds is always a problem; it is difficult to manufacture any instrument sensitive enough to register ordinary winds that is also strong enough to survive – let alone record accurately – winds of hurricane force.

Strangely, the centre, or "eye", of the hurricane (which can extend as much as fourteen miles across) often produces a sudden, eerie calm, preceded and followed by great and violent winds as the eye passes on. At that point the winds will reverse themselves completely; an area battered from the south will find itself attacked from the north as soon as the eye moves on. Stories are told of ships near land being deluged by flocks of birds, butterflies, and insects; caught helplessly in the swirl of the storm, they eventually find themselves blown to the centre and land on the boat as a temporary haven.

The folklore and legends of the people living around the Caribbean rim are full of traditional stories of hurricanes, but it was only with the arrival of Columbus that the area – and its perils – became known to Europeans. The lesson was not long in coming and was a dramatic one. In 1495, only three years after Columbus's historic voyage, a hurricane swept the recently named island of Santo Domingo; three Spanish ships riding at anchor there, preparing for the return voyage to Spain, were driven to the bottom of the sea. The surviving Spaniards adopted the local Caribbean word "huracán" for this terrifying phenomenon, and it soon spread through the vocabularies of the seafaring nations.

In 1605, Shakespeare – so familiar with nautical lore

that some respected authorities claim that he must have spent time at sea – referred in *Troilus and Cressida* to "the dreadful spout Which shipmen do the hurricano call". And some years later, Thomas Fuller, the dramatist, was using the word – "the winds are stark mad in a hurricano" – proving that in English the concept of hurricane was now well understood.

Through the centuries every sailor in the region feared the hurricane; booty-laden buccaneers slipping north to harbour safely in St. John's; wary Spanish skippers homeward bound from Cartagena; English slavers bringing in their human cargo from the Gold Coast; hardy Dutchmen sailing east from Surinam; Frenchmen on the sugar run from Martinique; Bluenose skippers out of Halifax with a load of codfish for the islands; Boston men in search of cotton from New Orleans – everyone who sailed these sunlit waters kept a careful weather eye open for the first sign of a hurricane.

The people of all races who inhabited the region came to terms with hurricanes. Their fatalism in the face of something they could neither prevent nor avoid is summed up by the spunky lady from the Alabama shore who, in 1976, told a *National Geographic* interviewer that she called her area "The Blackboard Coast" – because every few years a hurricane came and wiped it clean.

During the first fifty years of this century 358 hurricanes were tracked in the Western Atlantic, the Caribbean, and the Gulf of Mexico. While every one of them set palm trees whipping frenziedly, only twenty-five had even the slightest effect on Canada. For an Ontario resident, snugly nestled far from any sea, the word "hurricane" was a quaint, foreign one. Until October 1954.

CHAPTER TWO

TORONTO, 1954

It had rained all day. It had rained all week, but one day. Radio reports called for still more rain and followed up with the current popular hits of the day: "This Ole House", "The High and the Mighty", "Cross Over the Bridge". Rosemary Clooney, with two major hits, was perhaps the most-listened-to voice of the day, and, conscious of her position, had at first refused to record another fast-rising song, "C-monna My House", because she felt the lyrics were too suggestive.

It was October 15, 1954.

For Torontonians it was a fall day like any other – so wet and drizzly that people wondered aloud if the rain would ever stop – but otherwise, not a remarkable day. It would have been almost unthinkable to make any connection at all between the gathering momentum of the winds and the downpour of that Friday in Toronto and the wreckage and devastation left in exotic Haiti by a hurricane named "Hazel".

On Thursday there were no urgent storm warnings for Toronto. The headline news of that October 14 was "Oakville Ford on Strike". A newspaper story that same day told about Hazel heading west for the Carolinas at

5

130 miles per hour, but it probably merited no more than a casual glance. By Friday morning, local meteorologists may have been caught up in Hazel's progress, but most people were unaware of its approach. After all, this was Toronto in the early mid-1950s, a time of ebullience and confidence.

And why not! From its earliest beginnings as a French trading post, then, in 1793, as a fort to prevent U.S. invasion, and then as the new seat of government (a safer distance from the U.S. border than the former seat at Niagara-on-the-Lake), Toronto had weathered an American invasion, a popular uprising, and a major fire, and had sent hundreds of thousands of men to two world wars. Although the Second World War was still vivid in the minds of many Torontonians in 1954, most of them were busily engaged in making good in the converted frontier trading post that now stretched over 240 square miles around a north-shore harbour on Lake Ontario.

Originally a poor, threadbare community, not only did it have no trade, it actually passed a law against trade. Old records of 1800 carry an account of two men having been horsewhipped in Toronto for having indulged in trade as a private enterprise. A curiously incongruous note from history for a city that was to become the financial capital of the nation, with a third of the country's economic activity clustered within a fifty-mile radius of its heart.

In the fall of 1954 Torontonians were part of a brand new and highly innovative city structure. The Municipality of Metropolitan Toronto had been incorporated only the year before, and citizens were already familiar with the terminology – they spoke simply of "Metro". Metro was basically a collection of small villages, each with local loyalties and local concerns. In the boom of the postwar years, burgeoning growth in all directions had brought about a tangle of jurisdictions, and endless struggles on the part of small communities to meet ever-growing needs and demands. The City of Toronto proper wanted amalgamation; the suburbs, seeing themselves swallowed up and their identities lost, were adamantly opposed to the idea. The Honourable Leslie Frost, then Premier of Ontario, with the consummate balancing skill of a high-wire aerial artist, worked out the compromise that produced a miniature federation of the many parts. A provincial order in 1953 created the Municipality of Metropolitan Toronto, and thirteen communities were banded together in a supergovernment. Metro would deal with area-wide problems, but keep hands off local issues.

It was a unique form of government, one that attracted municipal experts from around the world, eager to come and see the system at work. And, appropriately for this new giant, the first chairman was a man of many attributes, not the least of which was considerable physical proportions. He was Frederick G. Gardiner and was almost immediately dubbed "Big Daddy".

Perhaps this compromise was very Canadian, very Toronto. On one hand was the desire for bigness and the efficiencies it could bring; on the other, the longing for the preservation of neighbourhoods. In the 1950s high-rise apartments were beginning to thrust their concrete-and-glass columns into the sky, but there were still far more clustered residential pockets, where quiet streets and modest homes spelled something approaching a village life. In fact, one area where homes were grand rather than modest called itself "Forest Hill Village". Throughout the rambling city there was a feeling of neatness, tidiness, a reflection of the WASP roots of the community.

The 1950s saw the beginnings of many changes in

Toronto. Although regularly accused by its detractors of being a cold, prim, unimaginative city of little flavour, it still attracted more Canadians from coast to coast than any other place in Canada. If the city had lived long by the Puritan work ethic that had earned it the pejoratively intended "Toronto the Good", the philosophy didn't seem to be working to its disadvantage in the fifties. It was a time of excitement, a time of building and growing and stretching of muscles.

The spring of 1954 had seen "Subway Day" (March 30) when the Yonge Street line became the first subway in all of Canada, with 4.6 miles of system that had cost $67 million and had taken four and a half years to build. The subway brought about more than advances in transportation; it brought an influx of Italian construction workers and the beginning of what was to become the largest Italian community outside of Italy. This marked one step in the postwar immigration process which was destined to change the complexion of a once predominantly British city to a cosmopolitan, multiracial metropolis. Soon there would be Portuguese, Poles, Germans, Hungarians, West Indians, Koreans – people from all over the world.

Abroad, the news that spring of 1954 was centred mainly on the Indochinese War and the last stages of the French army's fight to hold on to Dien Bien Phu. From early March, when a Vietminh army besieged Dien Bien Phu, until the fall of the great French fortress in May, newspapers the world over headlined the epic battle. The fall of Dien Bien Phu marked the end of the French colonial empire in Indochina, and, through subsequent agreements later in the year, the end of Indochina as a political entity. Cambodia, Laos, and Vietnam became completely independent, and one more Western state learned a harsh lesson about fighting a land war in Asia.

Ironically, *Time* magazine's "Man of the Year" for 1954 was U.S. Secretary of State John Foster Dulles, a leading cold warrior, who, in *Time*'s phrase, "reinforced the outposts".

It was the year of the first jet transport, the Boeing 707; and the new plane was almost immediately involved in a crash. The new British Comet also crashed. New technology brought the innovative air brakes, which reversed the thrust of jet engines to slow an aircraft on the runway. Studebaker and Packard, then major names in the auto industry, merged.

The top movies of the year were *Demetrius and the Gladiators*, with Victor Mature; *White Christmas*, with Bing Crosby; *The Glenn Miller Story*, with Jimmy Stewart; *A Star Is Born*; and *Magnificent Obsession*. A young actor named Marlon Brando was called a genius for his role in *On the Waterfront* and a great future was predicted for him. Other stars of the year were the veteran John Wayne (or so a 1954 article described him), Gina Lollobrigida, and Marilyn Monroe, who was in the news for her divorce from Joe DiMaggio, the baseball player.

It was not Joe DiMaggio's year in sport either, since the Yankee Clipper watched his team's rivals, the New York Giants, led by manager Leo Durocher and the outfielder Willie Mays, meet the favoured Cleveland Indians in the World Series. Cleveland had been favoured because of supposedly superior pitching, and because the team had won one hundred and eleven games during the season. But much of Cleveland's success had resulted from its playing in a weaker division, and the Giants swept the series in four straight games.

In golf a new face appeared on the scene. Arnold Palmer, a 24-year-old ex-coastguardsman, won the U.S. Amateur Golf Championship over Bob Sweeny, and began a love affair with golf fans that was to last for many years. In Canada, Marlene Stewart, a trim, poised young woman, made history by winning the third straight Canadian Women's Golf title in Dartmouth, Nova Scotia.

In 1954 Ernest Hemingway was awarded the Nobel prize for his work. For radio audiences in Toronto and beyond, Greg Clark and Gordon Sinclair remembered their days together as reporters on the *Toronto Daily Star*. Greg recalled, with wry humour, how often he read some of Hemingway's earlier stuff and counselled him that his writing was "too bumpy . . . too jerky . . . not smooth enough".

It was a year when the impossible suddenly became possible. Roger Bannister became the first man to run a four-minute mile. He did it on May 6, and the fact that he was a doctor, a pleasant-mannered man, intelligent and well spoken, made him the kind of hero who was tailor-made for a society out from under a world war and caught up in the new waves of optimism. Shortly after Bannister's record-shattering run, Australia's John Landy also cracked the four-minute barrier in a race in Finland. This set up the "Mile of the Century" in Vancouver, B.C., where Landy and Bannister were to meet in the British Empire Games. It proved to be an extraordinary race, run at a blistering pace from start to finish. On the final turn Landy was in the lead but the wall of sound put up by the ecstatic crowd meant that he could not hear where Bannister was. The Australian took a costly glance back over his inside shoulder to check on his opponent at precisely the moment that Bannister burst past on the outside. Landy was unable to catch him, but both men finished in under four minutes, the first time such a thing had ever happened. The race went down as one of the most exciting in sport history.

Vancouver, of course, was delighted. It had been a major triumph to get the Empire Games for the city. The coup was made possible by the building of the Empire Stadium, which at that time was the largest in Canada, with a capacity of 25,000. The stadium cost $1.5 million to build; in future it would seem like a bargain price.

It was the year of Canada–U.S. agreement on construction of a 3,000-mile radar warning system across the Canadian Arctic from Alaska to Greenland, and of the U.S. Supreme Court's ruling that racial segregation in the schools was unconstitutional. A controversy was raging over the novel idea that cigarette smoking might be a cause of cancer; and the best news on the medical front was of the anti-polio vaccine, developed by Dr. Jonas Salk, that was to affect the lives of millions and save the lives of many.

On the international scene, some of the major figures from the Second World War years still held power and prominence. Sir Winston Churchill was still Prime Minister of England; Pandit Nehru, Gandhi's son-in-law, was Prime Minister of India; General Eisenhower was President of the United States; Dag Hammarskjöld was Secretary-General of the United Nations; Konrad Adenauer was West Germany's Chancellor; and Pierre Mendès-France, a former Resistance fighter, was Premier of France. The People's Republic of China had the intelligent and enduring Chou En-lai as Foreign Minister, but his country, which held a quarter of the world's population, was not admitted to the United Nations.

"Uncle" Louis St. Laurent was Prime Minister of Canada, with Mike Pearson, who had participated in the original drafting of the U.N. Charter, as his Minister of External Affairs. The family-like designations of political leaders – "Uncle" Louis, "Big Daddy" Gardiner – perhaps suggest a simpler time, or at least one not filled with cynicism toward all political figures. That was to come later, as a bitter legacy of events such as the Watergate scandal and the resignation in disgrace of a President of the United States.

The early 1950s were years when the natural aftermath of a depression, a war, and then a postwar boom, brought with it a longing for things to be easier, for things to be fun again. It was the era of the hoola hoop, square dancing, and the very important teenager. Not that Toronto was exactly a swinging city. In 1950 much of the talk in the city was about the plebiscite on Sunday sport. But although clergymen railed from their pulpits about the evils of a pagan Sunday, the mood of the people was one of impatience with blue laws that governed, they thought, too much of their lives.

Money values were changing. A widow outside Toronto who sold a 65-acre farm for $145,000 lived to see the same property fetch $395,000 one year later. That was 1954. Yet 1950 saw one reputable periodical publish sample weekly budgets that showed how a family of four should manage on incomes of $45 and $80 a week. The lower figure was given as the average weekly wage that year, and the budget suggested the following: Food, $18 per week; Rent, $7.50; Fuel and Light, $2.25; Insurance and Savings, $2. If you were earning $80 a week they recommended: Food, $22 per week; Rent, $13.50; Fuel and Light, $3.50; Insurance and Savings, $10. Presumably the suggested budgets were drawn up for publication by a thrifty Toronto Scot.

Or perhaps Canadians generally were a thrifty lot at that particular time and place. For in 1952, 65 per cent of the cars owned in Canada were owned by families whose principal wage-earner was paid less than $3,000 a year; 40 per cent were owned by families where the annual income was less than $2,000 a year. Yet 66 per cent of those car-owners paid cash for their automobiles. The auto industry itself, including manufacturers, dealerships, and suppliers, gave work to 240,000 Canadians and had a payroll of $376 million. The auto not only provided jobs, transportation, and pleasure outings, but also a healthy chunk of tax revenue. The average excise and sales tax on an ordinary four-door sedan in 1952 was $362, as compared with $61 in 1939.

As it came up to Exhibition time in the summer of 1954, arrangements for the Duchess of Kent and Princess Alexandra to open the Canadian National Exhibition came under criticism. When rumours broke that the cost of the Royal visitors was to be $45,000, General Manager Hiram McCallum said the figures were wildly inaccurate but admitted that the cost would be higher than usual since the Duchess and her daughter would be accompanied by two ladies-in-waiting, an aide-de-camp, and three maids. Toronto, still euphoric over the 1951 visit of Princess Elizabeth and her Greek Prince Charming, seemed, on balance, to regard the Royal expense as justified.

That month, fur sales, traditional in August, featured Northern Back Muskrat coats, mink-dyed at $187; Persian Lamb, $387; Plucked Otter, an extravagant $977. Among the prices featured in newspaper grocery ads were: prime rib of beef, 45 cents a pound; blade, short rib, and shoulder, 35 cents a pound; bread, sliced or unsliced, 15 cents; and milk in a sanitized quart carton, 20 cents. In Ottawa, the nation's capital, the two English dailies, the *Journal* and the *Citizen*, daringly boosted the price of Saturday editions to ten cents from five.

On Tuesday, August 10, a dynamite blast touched off the much-heralded $600 million St. Lawrence power project, while Premier Frost of Ontario and Governor Thomas Dewey took part in double ceremonies on the Canadian and U.S. sides of the river at Cornwall and Massena, New York. The blast exploded the first earth for a power project which by 1958 was scheduled to send out 12.6 billion kilowatts a year to be shared by Canada and the United States. People favoured the St. Lawrence Seaway and power development, but for some seven thousand residents affected when the twenty thousand acres of farmland were to be covered by floodwaters, there was understandable regret. To be wholly or partially flooded were towns such as Mille Roches, Moulinette, Wales, Dickinsons Landing, Farrans Point, Aultsville, Morrisburg, East Williamsburg, and Iroquois, many of them founded around 1780 by Loyalists fleeing from the south.

That August saw flooding that was not man-made, and not to any good practical purpose, in other parts of the world. In what was then referred to as Mainland China, or Red China, a flood destroyed much of the Chinese food supply as the country lost 67 per cent of its farmland to floodwaters. Peking radio reports told of the Yangtze River rising to the highest level in a hundred years. Broadcasts within that country called on its people for a strong effort to "surmount natural calamity".

In the Toronto area, natural calamity seemed a world away. That fall of 1954 a home-grown heroine was about to be born, and she would deserve every crazy, frenzied, worshipful tribute that would come her way. Before the Second World War, the CNE had been the backdrop for the famous Wrigley Swims in Lake Ontario. Together with the Toronto *Telegram*, the CNE organizers dreamed up the idea of highlighting the 1954 fair by inviting the internationally known California marathon swimmer, Florence Chadwick, thirty-four, to swim across Lake Ontario. She would receive $2,500 for tackling the swim and $7,500 more if she were victorious. It was not a "race" in any sense of the word; it was a question of whether the American swimmer could stand not only the distance, but the notoriously cold water of Lake Ontario.

Marilyn Bell, a freckle-faced sixteen-year-old, only five foot two and 119 pounds, and Winnie Roach Leuszler, a 28-year-old from St. Thomas, Ontario, challenged Miss Chadwick – and so was launched the drama of Lake Ontario, with all the elements of a movie thriller. Local girls *versus* the American visitor; sponsored famous guest pitted against the young and uninvited.

The Toronto *Telegram*, somewhat disconcerted by a fine promotion gone askew, at first refused to recognize the unofficial challengers. At that point the *Toronto Daily Star* jumped on the bandwagon and announced in banner headlines that it would underwrite the challengers' expenses and arrange for boats to accompany the two Canadian girls. Even before it started the entire swim had become a cause célèbre, with the rivalry of the two papers lending considerable fuel to the controversy about who had the right to swim "our" lake; in the course of the swim the rivalry between the two papers led to comical acts of near-piracy, while the rivalry on shore reached almost violent proportions. Some CNE officials, out of genuine concern, questioned whether the lake was any place for a youngster of the tender age of sixteen.

The course of the swim was from Youngstown, New York, to the breakwater in front of the Canadian National Exhibition, an actual distance of twenty-one miles – if you could travel a straight line through the water. Winnie Roach Leuszler made two false starts, and on the second was rescued from the water sobbing and only half conscious. Florence Chadwick battled waves that reached twelve feet in height, nausea that persisted hour after hour, until, exhausted and weakened, she too was hauled out of the water.

Marilyn Bell, who began her swim just after 11:00 p.m., September 8, swam continuously, sometimes in almost a state of shock, throughout the blackness of the night. As she swam she had to contend with the terrors of the silent eels that attached themselves to her, with the nausea that came from the rough seas, and with the numbing cold. Throughout the next day, she swam on towards the Toronto shore.

The sixteen-year-old's courage captured the imagination of the entire city. Headlines and breathless newscasts seemed to continue nonstop during the many hours of the swim. Radio, able to bulletin her progress almost minute by minute, fed the tension and excitement, and an entire city was caught up in suspense. In the hours of dusk, a crowd of 100,000 had gathered at the lakeshore, anxiously, eagerly waiting. Marilyn did not disappoint them. At 8:06 p.m., after twenty-one hours in the water, she reached out and touched the concrete of the CNE breakwater with her left hand. Gus Ryder, her coach, and a reporter pulled her into the boat and she was rushed, dazed and exhausted, to the peace and quiet of a warm bed.

For Canada, Marilyn's swim was the same kind of dazzling achievement as Roger Bannister's four-minute mile in the spring of that year. The first person ever to swim Lake Ontario, she had swum thirty-two miles in just under twenty-one hours. Everyone happily embarked on a veritable binge of Marilyn-worship, and no young heroine ever met the adulation and acclaim with more grace and modesty. Sponsored or not, she was reputed to have collected $50,000 in prizes and gifts, very tangible tributes.

September 1954 brought something else for many Canadians to feel happy about. The Defence department announced that two-thirds of the Canadian troops in Korea would be home by Christmas, or the end of the year. The 2nd Battalion of the Black Watch, the 3rd Regiment of the Royal Canadian Horse Artillery, and the 4th Battalion of the Canadian Guards would disengage in that order and return home. The destroyer *Cayuga*, patrolling Korean waters since early June, would also be homeward bound, leaving the *Iroquois* and the *Huron* still on active duty under United Nations command.

That summer of 1954 Canadians were still trying to explain themselves – or were they seeking an identity? *Montreal Star* editor George Ferguson told a New York audience that Americans knew very little about us because we gave them very little reason to want to know more about us.

"We behave ourselves, and have a tradition of law and order which surpasses yours. . . . Our divorce rate is much lower than yours, we stay much at home, we go to church on Sundays in surprisingly large numbers, and, taken all round, we are a respectable lot – respectable, but inclined to be dull. Our virtues and our vices alike are pedestrian. We lack vividness and colour and violent emotion. Even though we know more or less where we are going, we trudge toward our destination. We do not skip or run. We lack both bands and flags on our national journey.

"We seldom surprise ourselves, and it is therefore hardly to be expected that we will surprise outsiders," he said with modesty. "We lack instability, which is always an interesting quality, even when it is most annoying," Ferguson told his American listeners, allowing that we did however have the capacity to be good neighbours.

One might be forgiven for wondering at the reaction of that same audience if they happened upon the retired Ottawa correspondent of the *New York Times*, newsman Percy Phillip, and listened to his quite serious account of his two-hour conversation with the Canadian Prime Minister Mackenzie King, who had been dead for four years. And would they find that late Prime Minister's penchant for his own talks with the dead, for séances and crystal balls, compatible with Mr. Ferguson's description of Canadians?

If we didn't have the bands and flags Mr. Ferguson spoke of that fall of 1954 for our "national journey", our country highways had one rather distinctive Canadian feature – the moose. The moose population had grown to such proportions that the animals had become a traffic hazard. Ontario's Department of Lands and Forests issued some useful advice for motorists finding themselves fender to face with a moose: slam on the brakes, but don't blow the horn. While not pretending to have knowledge of moose language, the Department volunteered the theory that the moose interprets the blast as some kind of challenge and usually charges the cars, with unfortunate results all round.

It was a time marked by one of the hottest political duels of the country. Federal *versus* provincial rights formed the battleground, and the protagonists were Prime Minister Louis St. Laurent, the first French-Canadian prime minister since 1911, and Quebec's Premier Maurice Duplessis. When Duplessis refused federal grants for education and highways and flatly rejected Ottawa's tax agreements, which had been accepted by all other provincial premiers, Uncle Louis, speaking on Quebec territory, did not mince words. "I am just launching a campaign on education. The people of Quebec have been misled too long by a group of political dummies, raising scarecrows and taking sidetracks to confuse the real issue."

Duplessis, on his part, interpreted the federal government's motives as a desire to control provincial education, thus playing on French Canadians' fears of Anglo-Saxon domination and the loss of their culture. To make up the finances lost by his stand, the Quebec premier imposed a provincial income tax of 15 per cent on Quebec wage-earners and loudly laid the blame for it at Ottawa's door.

When a compromise was finally struck, ending a bitter feud between the two men, each claimed a victory. Quebec lowered its provincial income tax from the announced 15 per cent to 7.5 per cent and Ottawa upped its tax deduction allowance to all the provinces to 7.5 per cent, thus avoiding double taxation in Quebec. It was the kind of exercise that was to become increasingly familiar in the years that lay ahead.

Still, Canada was feeling its prosperity, and that year saw the beginnings of a plan to establish the Canada Council for the Encouragement of the Arts, Letters, Humanities, and Social Sciences. The much-acclaimed Massey Report of 1951 had recommended such a body, but some saw many political complications. The idea of state-sponsored culture was unappealing to certain cabinet ministers, and others raised the spectre of provincial annoyance, particularly Quebec's, at the federal government meddling in their affairs. Culture groups lobbied effectively for help and support and finally the fall of 1954 saw a committee of four cabinet ministers charged with the responsibility of bringing in the workable plan. They hoped to adopt the legislation in January at the opening of the next session of Parliament.

It was a time of concern for education, and one of the surest ways of starting an argument was to begin discussion of Dr. Hilda Neatby's controversial book *So Little for the Mind*. Dr. Neatby, a Saskatchewan history professor, had written a blistering indictment of Canadian education in which she accused the school system of having adopted an artificial modernity and of having lost sight of the true intellectual purposes of schools. While many agreed with her thesis, the wrath that descended upon her would have enabled her to compile a veritable dictionary of uncomplimentary adjectives, all applied to her. She was called abusive, acid, angry, arrogant, peevish, pitiful, prejudiced, tendentious . . . the criticisms seemed endless. But the debate was useful at a time when people's interests had returned to home base, to children, family, togetherness, and all the concerns that went with a more relaxed, more affluent time, a period of boom and development.

Canadians were enjoying that boom. The early 1950s had seen the Old Age Security and Old Age Assistance Acts become operative. Before the decade was out, Canada's gross national product would double, from $18 billion to $36 billion, and we would go from being one of the iron-ore importing countries to one of the world's great exporters of it. There would be $60 billion worth of new housing starts within the decade, as people pursued the dream of a home of their own.

There was money to spend for houses, clothes, refrigerators and TV sets, and, yes, travel. In 1954 there were twenty-three million visits to the United States by Canadians, who spent $307 million or an average per capita of $20.79. In fact, we outspent our American neighbours that year by $25 million. While there were twenty-eight million visits northward by our American neighbours, their total spending here that year was $282 million.

In Toronto, television was just beginning its continuous struggle to put a Canadian stamp on entertainment and information. Wayne and Shuster, Andrew Allan, J. B. McGeachy, Joyce Hahn, Mart Kenney, Norma Locke, Dick MacDougal, Percy Saltzman, and Elaine Grand were among the early Canadian television stars. Wayne and Shuster, in fact, were destined for the phenomenal kind of career that would span several decades and win them acclaim for the most frequent appearances of any act on the Ed Sullivan show. Remarkably, they escaped the lure of a permanent move to the entertainment world of the United States. Howard Cable, Byng Whitteker, Juliette, Joan Fairfax, and Denny Vaughan, many of whom worked in both radio and television, were others who took part in the electronic revolution in Canada that was changing family patterns, giving rise to meals in front of the TV and family arguments about what program to watch. Kate Aitken, that undisputed woman champion of a thousand activities, held court on both CBC and CFRB radio several times a day and did television commercials on the side. A veritable whirlwind of a woman who sometimes arrived breathless at a studio having careered from airport to radio station to the accompaniment of a screaming motorcycle escort, she juggled broadcasting, writing, Canadian National Exhibition administrative chores, public speaking, and world travel in a manner never seen before or since. Fellow broadcaster Gordon Sinclair once estimated that 32 percent of all Canadians listened to one or another of her radio programs in the 1950s.

Radio was a comfortable habit that had become firmly established by the regular newscasts all during the war; television was the newcomer in the 1950s – at least the Canadian programming was – and the shows of the evening before were often grist for the conversational mill of each day.

When the Toronto Argonauts played the Ottawa Rough Riders on a weekend in September 1954, it was the first telecast of a football game in Canadian history. It was the year the Edmonton Eskimos won the Grey Cup. Or, some would say, the year it was "lost" by the Montreal Alouettes. In the last few seconds of the game Chuck Hunsinger fumbled the ball away on Edmonton's ten-yard line. Jackie Parker picked up the loose ball and raced ninety yards for the tying touchdown, which, when converted, gave the Eskimos a controversial one-point victory. It was a game football enthusiasts would recount to one another for years to come.

And it was the year the Detroit Red Wings, led by Gordie Howe, Terry Sawchuk, and Red Kelly, beat the Montreal Canadiens, and their up-and-coming stars Jean Beliveau and Doug Harvey, four games to three to win the Stanley Cup. Toronto fans watched in dismay as the Maple Leafs, the perennial Stanley Cup winners in the late 1940s, fell off the pace and failed to make the finals.

But if one Canadian institution was ailing, another was springing to life. In the small town of Stratford, Ontario, a theatrical dream had been born – the Stratford Shakespearean Festival, housed in a mammoth tent overlooking a tranquil river complete with swans. The beginning might be modest, but the vision was one of grandeur, of a festival of world calibre and a theatre that would one day know no need to showcase classical actors from abroad, but would give nourishment and growing space to Canada's best in the company of the world's best.

In Toronto it was a time of beginnings: of the Golden Mile of new factories; of the Avro Arrow program with all its inspirational hopes for a new and major aircraft industry; of a new focus on Toronto harbour and its facilities in light of the St. Lawrence Seaway; and the boast that Toronto was the fastest-growing city in North America.

While the rest of the country looked on, the importance of Toronto's stock exchange, television production centre, corporate headquarters, banks and other financial groups, ad agencies, and educational and cultural institutions of all sorts grew year after year. Naturally, that didn't change the almost traditional "hate Toronto" feeling elsewhere. Surely some future psychologist will have a field day analysing the ambiguity of attitude of Canadians generally, and many Torontonians too, towards what was to be the largest city in the nation. In another decade altogether, the Honourable John Robarts, Co-Chairman of the Task Force on Canadian Unity, was to say, with possibly as much truth as rueful humour, that the most unifying thing in Canada was its hatred of Toronto. But in 1954 the constant and steady influx of people from every corner of the Dominion, and from every country of the world, had already begun. The weaving of a rich ethnic tapestry that would give a variety of cultures, cuisines, and attitudes to the city was under way.

Despite the Cold War, it seemed a time of innocence and goodwill. Laudatory and favourable magazine pieces, a whole series of them, were running on the RCMP. Under headings like "The Public's Own Private Eye" or "Their Thirty-Year War with the Commies", the stories told us what Canadians already knew and believed, that our federal police force was indeed worthy of being a special kind of national symbol. No other country in the world portrayed its policemen as one of its most glamorous tourist attractions. The sad revelations of the 1970s were a long way off.

Many of the concerns of the day centred on the young, and on life in the suburbs. June Callwood, already a perceptive and sensitive writer, was doing pieces like "Will Your Youngster Turn to Crime?" and "Seventeen Hours in an Emergency Ward". As evidence of an awakened interest in the North, the fall of 1954 saw *Maclean's* magazine feature a special issue on the Canadian North with a major article by its Managing Editor, Pierre Berton, who had travelled twenty thousand miles for background on the general story.

In Ottawa, Blair Fraser was writing optimistically that post office authorities hoped there would be an improvement in the Canadian postal service before the end of the summer. Steps had been taken, and other steps contemplated, which they believed would arrest the deterioration in the Canadian mails that had begun about three years earlier. He traced the history of the decline from 1951, when the government decided to cut mail delivery from twice to once a day and put a thousand postmen out of jobs. The post office fought these moves, because of the addition of so many new housing developments in the Ottawa–Montreal–Toronto triangle. But the Department of Finance and the Opposition were adamant about the cuts, which they said would save $3 million annually. A strangely quiescent public said very little. The days of almost certain next-day delivery within the triangle, and often between Winnipeg and the Triangle, were gone forever.

The cut-back also tells us something significant about government attitude to expenditures in 1954. For Canada, it was the first year national production was down since the end of the war. Cost of living rose two points. But there were 5 million Canadians employed at unprecedentedly high wages and 175,000 unemployed. While there was talk of a possible deficit ahead, 1954 was, in fact, a remarkably good year. The string of postwar surpluses that often ran to the hundreds of millions was not yet at an end, and the Canadian dollar stood at $1.03 U.S. Canadian Savings Bonds were advertised as good investments, paying 3.25 per cent. The brief slowdown that marked 1953-54 was quickly followed by further rapid expansion of the economy. And as late in the decade as 1957, with the stunning election win by the Conservatives, the federal coffers still had a surplus in the neighbourhood of $400 million.

In 1954 beauty contests raised not one word of protest or controversy. That August, Barbara Joan Markham, a Cornwall, Ontario, art student, won the annual Miss Canada contest, to the applause of all who watched the competition in Windsor. Miss Markham, a brunette, stood 5 feet 9½ inches tall, weighed 145 pounds, and measured 37-26-37.

Significantly absent from news records of the day is the word "separatism". Political stories concerning Quebec tended to deal with investigations into crime. The prosecuting attorney for the Montreal Crime Commission, a 38-year-old lawyer named Jean Drapeau, was campaigning for the position of Mayor on the platform "Clean Up City Hall". The long investigation into vice in the city dragged on for three years and was thought by many to have become an expensive and useless bore. It cost $400,000 and resulted in a host of dismissals and fines.

Much more exciting was the version of early Canadian history that everyone could enjoy in *Maclean's* magazine, which was running the serialized version of Thomas B. Costain's *The White and the Gold*. Costain, Brantford born, went on to edit *Maclean's* before leaving the magazine and Canada in the 1920s to work and write in the U.S., where he eventually became an American citizen. His writing, however, often reflected his Canadian background. By 1954 his books had already sold seven million copies in Canada and the U.S.; *The Black Rose* had been translated into eighteen languages and, along with *The Silver Chalice*, had been the subject of a feature film.

In short, 1954 was a good year to be in Canada, a good year to be in Toronto. It was a time of uncomplicated ambitions for the house with the picture window in front and the garden in back. If you were lucky, you might have a barbecue and patio, and some even aspired to a swimming pool. The togetherness theme of the postwar baby-boom era was still in vogue, and an enormous amount of attention was being paid to teenagers, their likes, dislikes, music, and dress. Spike heels, seamed nylons, strapless gowns, and crinolines were in, as were bobby socks and penny loafers. Jo Stafford, Eddie Fisher, and Doris Day were big names in pop music, and the fact that there was a musical group called "The Crewcuts" speaks volumes about the look of the period. People were reading *The Robe* and Igor Gouzenko's *Fall of a Titan*, and chortling about the latest outrageous commentaries on radio of "Rawhide", otherwise known as young Max Ferguson.

In fact, the only element to dampen the Canadian mood was the wet weather. It was one of the rainiest years in Canadian history. In the West, which had once known the ravages of dustbowl years, heavy rain so damaged wheat crops that the harvest was the smallest since 1937. In Quebec, rain brought industrial building to a standstill. In the Ottawa area, potatoes were left unharvested and fall ploughing could not be done because of mud and water. Southern Ontario, and in particular the Toronto region, was not exempt from this wet-weather pattern. Toronto, with its finger-like ravines and valleys reaching down towards Lake Ontario, was waterlogged.

The Greater Toronto area is made up of flat tablelands stretching northward to the more rugged Muskoka and Haliburton Highlands areas with their abundance of rocky outcroppings, hills, and lakes. The flat landscape of Greater Toronto tilts gently as it extends northward; and that tableland, much of it clay that cannot absorb water, is veined with many streams, creeks, and rivers, like the spokes of a wheel, all draining south into Lake Ontario. In ordinary times, the ravines that cradle those rivers are treasured patches of unspoiled greenbelt that attract adventurous children and outdoor-loving adults. The rivers are usually placid, slow-moving little streams that curl their way lazily through the valleys and down to the lake.

But this October the streams were all running high.

The rain, which seemed interminable, was doing its customary job of washing down silt and eroding the banks, until all the rivers and creeks were running brown as coffee, so that great pools of darkened river water stained the lake where they entered. Each valley was acting like a great funnel, carrying off the tons of rainwater and along with it earth, silt, and pieces of debris, sticks, twigs, and the like. It was all very unusual for fall, much more like the spring run-off. Unusual, but hardly dangerous.

Though people talked of the rain and grumbled about it, longing for the usual crisp, sunny October days, no one foresaw the disaster that rain could mean. But, as Hurricane Hazel headed north, the stage was set for one of the most bizarre chapters in Toronto's history.

CHAPTER THREE

THE PATH OF THE STORM

It all began with a puff of wind causing a ripple on the surface of the Atlantic near the point where that ocean becomes the Caribbean. In time the wind grew until the ripples became waves and the waves became whitecaps, driven into spindrift by the freshening gale. At that point, on October 5, 1954, Hurricane Hazel was officially born near the island of Grenada, not far from the coast of South America. U.S. Navy "hurricane hunters" from the Naval Air Station in Jacksonville, Florida, were the first to spot the new storm, and duly reported it. Because in its initial stages the storm moved slowly, these Navy fliers were to spend a record 207 hours keeping their eyes on her as Hazel swept through the Caribbean and the Atlantic.

Hazel was not the first, but the eighth, tropical storm that year. In accordance with long tradition, all of the hurricanes were given girls' names as if to domesticate them; each year, too, the names were given in alphabetical order. Thus Hurricane Alice inaugurated the 1954 series on June 25, when it struck the coast of Mexico near Texas and helped to cause disastrous Rio Grande floods. Barbara blew out harmlessly between July 28 and 30.

Then, Carol, the year's worst for the United States, began moving up the Florida coast on August 26; it picked up speed and headed northward, sweeping over Long Island and the New England states on August 31, causing sixty-eight deaths, and property damage of $500 million. Carol was followed by Hurricane Dolly, which also took the northern route but remained far out to sea, on September 1 and 2; by Edna (September 6 to 12), which killed eleven people and caused property damage in New England; by Florence (September 12), which went across the Gulf of Mexico, causing minor damage in Mexico and Texas; by Gilda (September 26 and 27), which followed the same route as Florence, causing little damage; and then by Hazel.

Hazel was to go down in the records as "the most erratic hurricane in history", according to the American Weather Bureau. On October 6, 7, and 8, Hazel slowly moved westward, gathering strength as it moved along parallel to the Venezuelan coast. On October 9, Hazel turned north and followed a course north by northwest. On October 10 and 11, Hazel headed north by northeast, towards Haiti.

Haiti forms the western half of an island shared with the Dominican Republic; it has two peninsulas, a long one and a short one, pointing west like the claws of a crab. On the southern peninsula there are two major towns: Aux Cayes, the third-largest city of the island republic, with a population of some 30,000, a bustling seaport for the export of rum, coffee, cocoa, bananas, rice, and sugar; and Jérémie, the second-largest city on the peninsula. Port-au-Prince, the capital, though also on the coast, is well protected because of its location between the two peninsulas.

On October 12, Hurricane Hazel, now fully developed, hit the southern peninsula of Haiti with vicious

force. Probably no country on earth could have withstood
the winds of 115 miles per hour, but Haiti, a poor, back-
ward country ruled by "Papa Doc" Duvalier and his cult
of voodoo, was hopelessly ill-equipped to face Hazel.
Many of the buildings on the island were tightly packed
to accommodate the population density of four hundred
people to the square mile; and the buildings themselves,
palm lath covered over with plaster and roofed with tin,
were pitiful targets for the hurricane. Wind-whipped seas
pummelled the coastal towns and levelled most of their
buildings. The wind tossed around their remnants like so
many newspapers in a breeze, and metal roofs flying
through the air mowed down any person unlucky enough
to be in their path. Tough fronds of palm became razor-
like weapons sent whistling through the air by the keen-
ing winds. Hills that had been covered by trees before the
storm were left absolutely bare, looking as though a forest
fire had denuded the mountainside. People said afterwards that the very ground itself was hot from the friction
of the winds.

In Aux Cayes frightened people sought sanctuary in
the Catholic church, the largest, strongest building in the
town; but it too was flattened by the winds and horizon-
tal sheets of rain. One couple whose house had blown
away were seeking shelter, the man carrying their baby
son clutched to his chest, when the wind tore the infant
from his arms. The frantic couple spent most of the night
out in the hurricane searching for the child. Next day
they found the baby, blown underneath the wreckage of
a building. The child was unharmed.

The toll of dead was not easy to assess at once but an
early figure given is two hundred, and thousands were
without even the simple shelter they had known. The
town of Jérémie was reported to have been almost swept
into the sea. The Haitian Red Cross sent out an appeal

for help and within two days President Eisenhower had pledged aid, and the U.S. aircraft carrier *Saipan* soon anchored in the Jérémie harbour. Helicopters from the *Saipan* began the delivery of medicine, food, and clothing for the victims of the hurricane.

Canadian missionaries there at the time recall that some of the first batches of food dropped were packaged cake mixes; the native Haitians, accustomed to making a particular type of dumpling with ordinary flour, were somewhat astonished by the curious sweetness of the cake mixes. And the missionaries were left to marvel at the choice of food packages, many of which never did reach proper destinations because of local graft. CARE was reputed to have done the best job during the emergency; they themselves cooked, prepared, and served individual meals.

For an island where poverty was normal at the best of times (the average annual income was $100), the devastation of the hurricane was awesome. It demolished not only shelter, but gardens and plantations which meant much to a fragile economy where food was always scarce.

But this was hurricane territory. Hurricanes were not an unfamiliar enemy. And there had been warnings about Hazel. Though not much was possible in the way of preparations or defence, there had at least been provision for supplies of fresh water, since from bitter past experience the islanders knew that the flooding and the death of animals would contaminate water supplies. They were right, and another of the consequences of Hazel in Haiti was an outbreak of typhoid.

But this was in the future; for the present, Hazel was on the move again. On October 13, the hurricane began to move northwest through the gentle, low-lying Bahamas, picking up more speed and apparently heading for Florida.

On October 14, Hazel missed Florida by three hundred miles, but began to threaten the coast of South Carolina. It was the story of this possibility that first made an appearance in Toronto papers, although, of course, there was no hint or suggestion of any connection between that hurricane threat and the Toronto area.

The first news story about Hazel to appear in the venerable *New York Times* was on October 13, and it rated five paragraphs on page 17. It dealt with the storm damage to Haiti the day before. The next day the Haiti story hit the front page of the *New York Times*. The weather forecast that day said that New York City would experience light, variable winds, while western New York State could expect showers and thunderstorms. To the south, people were inclined to take things a little more seriously. Eighty U.S. naval vessels hastily put out to sea from Norfolk, Virginia, to ride out the storm in open water; and military planes scrambled for safety to airports as far away as Kansas. Meanwhile the Canadian escort vessel H.M.C.S. *Digby*, bound for Esquimalt *via* Panama, was playing hide and seek with the storm. The Chaplain, the Reverend W. Donald Goodger, remembers their decision to shelter from Hazel in Cuba, and then to run through the outer winds of the hurricane to Jamaica. Some days later, calling home to Ayr, Ontario, Mr. Goodger was astonished to find that Ontario knew all about the tropical storm he had encountered near Jamaica.

By Thursday, October 15, the North American news media were more alert to the danger represented by Hazel, which for ten days had been just another storm in someone else's backyard. At 2:00 a.m. the U.S. Weather Bureau warned that the New York area "will be in for a rough day today". At exactly the same time, the Miami Weather Bureau said there were some indications that Hazel was swinging westward, and might strike the coast near Charleston, S.C., and pass inland. The same Miami bulletin predicted it could arrive in eastern Pennsylvania by afternoon, and eastern New York by nightfall.

At that time Hazel's winds were clocked at one hundred miles per hour, and the blast extended some two hundred miles from the centre of the hurricane to the north and east, and one hundred miles to the south and west. The American Red Cross alerted all of its chapters from Savannah, Georgia, to the Chesapeake Bay area.

At 8:00 a.m. that Friday, Hazel was forty miles southwest of Myrtle Beach, South Carolina – that pleasant resort town that annually draws Canadian visitors by the thousands for golf and a break from Canadian weather during the later winter months. Hazel picked up speed, veered slightly to the west, and at 9:15 crossed the coast just east of Myrtle Beach.

This first assault on the North American mainland was dramatic, bringing howling winds of 100 to 120 miles an hour and tides 9 to 11 feet above normal. In some places the tides were over 17 feet above mean low water. As a result every fishing dock on the 170-mile stretch of shore from Myrtle Beach to Cedar Island, N.C., was destroyed. Debris borne by the storm, and later found along the coast, included such odd things as coconuts, pieces of bamboo, large tropical clams weighing as much as eight pounds, and ironically, a mahogany bowl with "Made in Haiti" stamped on the bottom.

Along the coast of South Carolina, in Cherry Grove, Windy Hill, Ocean Drive, and Caroline Beaches, homes, hotels, and public buildings were flattened; streets were awash; the four-storey Breakers Hotel had its roof torn off, and its walls collapsed.

As the hours went by, Hazel raced northward. All along the North Carolina coast the storm took a terrible toll, from Cape Fear to Cape Hatteras. Even inland, at

Wilmington, N.C., three freighters were torn from their moorings, while the flat, pleasant coast lands to the north were devastated.

On into "tidewater Virginia" swept the storm. The great port of Norfolk was almost empty of naval vessels, but two men lost their lives there, electrocuted by felled power lines. The *Newport News* of Virginia faced the very odd situation of a major local story it couldn't get into print; the tall brick chimney of the news plant had toppled, demolishing the composing room. On up through Virginia, past historic Williamsburg and the ground where Lee's and Grant's men fought and died, the path of the storm could easily be followed by the trail of broken windows, roofless barns, tangled power lines, flooded streets, and floating buildings. In Fredericksburg (a later AP report noted with glee) the city council had just authorized the employment of a commercial rainmaker when the heavy rains spawned by Hazel poured down on the city.

It was between 6:00 and 6:30 p.m. when the storm hit Washington. Friday at 6:30 is perhaps the busiest time of the week in a city that abounds in diplomatic receptions and dinner parties, rich in political lore and gossip. It's the time when those in town usually have at least one engagement to keep, while others make excuses and seek the peace of country weekends. This Friday, things were very different. Unlike many large American cities with high, jagged skyscraper profiles, Washington is full of low, squat, solid government buildings, and most of these were emptied of their thousands of civil servants early in the afternoon. The Civil Service Commission, always conscious of the traffic crush at the Potomac bridges, had directed an early closing to avoid a calamitous traffic jam at the height of the storm. Schools had gotten the word, too. The result was that while Hurricane Hazel whirled around the Washington Monument and crashed against the front of the White House, much of Washington sat out the storm in the relative safety of their own homes, wondering when the power would be resumed. Despite the city's readiness, two were killed and thirty-six injured.

By 7:00 p.m. the hurricane was carving its crazy path north through Maryland, Delaware, and Pennsylvania, with winds diminished only slightly to eighty-four miles per hour. By 7:00 p.m. New Yorkers were cursing the rain, and in the city where it's always difficult to get a cab at rush hour, this night many cabs were simply refusing to move at all. By 7:45 the rain was a torrential downpour that set strangers huddling together in doorways discussing whether to wait it out or make a break for home. The winds were fifty-five to sixty miles per hour. The centre of the storm passed, whirling and screaming, 150 miles west of New York City and headed north through Pennsylvania and upper New York State.

At 11:00 p.m. the U.S. Weather Bureau felt able to take Hazel out of its hurricane class since the winds had dropped below seventy-four miles per hour. But Hazel was headed out over Lake Ontario towards a city that had never known even a slowing hurricane, in an area where no hurricane had a logical right to be, on a path unheard of for a tropical storm.

CHAPTER FOUR

A CITY UNPREPARED

Did people know that Hurricane Hazel was coming, that it posed a genuine threat to the Toronto area?

Today, many will claim that it was the best-kept secret in town; others will claim with equal force that it was a fully documented meteorological event that should have taken nobody by surprise. Paradoxically, both impressions contain a great deal of truth.

At 6:00 a.m., Friday, October 15, 1954, W. E. (Fred) Turnbull, Officer in Charge at the Malton Dominion Public Weather Office, reported for a briefing. He was surprised to find that his colleague Norman Grundy had just completed a prognostic chart that showed Hurricane Hazel over the eastern section of Lake Ontario by 2300 Eastern Standard Time. To reach this position, the hurricane centre would have to accelerate rapidly and follow an unprecedented course. The acceleration was what one might expect, but for a hurricane reaching the Cape Hatteras area to move across the Allegheny Mountains, following a north to northwest course, was unexpected.

Norman Grundy's analysis of the situation and his reasoning seemed flawless, however, and after consultation with the shift supervisor, he proceeded to issue his

forecast for release at 9:30 a.m. On the basis of his pro-
posed chart, that forecast called for continuous rain
throughout Friday and Friday night.

Before leaving his shift at 8:30, Mr. Grundy had a
routine telephone call from the Toronto *Telegram*. During
the course of this interview he stated that the hurricane
was moving northward towards Ontario, and present indications were that it would continue on this northerly
course, arriving over Lake Ontario about midnight. He
predicted that the hurricane would diminish in intensity,
but that in any case the heavy rain then falling (there
had been an inch since 6:00 a.m.) would continue
throughout Friday night.

In his written report of that day, Fred Turnbull
states, "The issuing of a weather bulletin, particularly
advising of the approach of a hurricane, is a serious step
and not to be taken lightly. Since storms of this nature
seldom follow our predicted course, and rarely travel 700
miles overland retaining sufficient energy to be alarming,
we decided to consult our Central Analysis Office in
Montreal before issuing a special bulletin. In a telephone
call to Montreal, Mr. Leaver of the Central Analysis
Office agreed to have his staff give special consideration
to Hurricane Hazel, and call us immediately after com-
pletion of their prognostic chart."

Between 9:30 and 10:00 a.m., a *Telegram* reporter
called a second time, seeking a progress report on the
hurricane and more specific interpretation of the rain
prediction. Mr. Turnbull advised the reporter that he
couldn't give specific amounts, but that the 24-hour rainfall (Friday, 6:00 a.m., to Saturday, 6:00 a.m.) *could well
be the heaviest ever recorded in the city's history*. When asked
what the record was, Mr. Turnbull said, "Close to four
inches, back in 1887."

This call prompted Fred Turnbull to discuss with Dr.

McTaggart-Cowan, Chief of the Forecast Division, the issuance of an immediate official bulletin. He believed the *Telegram* would feature a hurricane story and felt that in fairness to the general public, an official statement should be issued then and there. As a result, the following special weather bulletin was prepared, addressed to all news services. The bulletin was transmitted over private teletype network, sent by phone to local radio stations and to commercial concerns appearing on the weather office's severe-weather warning list, and telegraphed to all Marconi radio stations for broadcast in "clear" to all vessels operating on the Great Lakes.

"Hurricane Hazel moved inland near Myrtle Beach, South Carolina, this morning. Highest winds are estimated at 100 miles per hour over a small area, with winds of 40 to 60 miles per hour extending out 80 miles to the North and East and 40 miles to the South and West of the centre. Hurricane Hazel is expected to continue at 35 to 40 miles per hour towards the Northwest for the next few hours, then to follow a more Northerly course.

"The present Northerly motion of the hurricane centre is causing considerable apprehension in Southern Ontario areas. In this respect, it should be remembered that the Allegheny mountain range lies between us and the storm centre. The mountain range may break up, or materially weaken the storm's intensity, or cause it to veer off towards the Northeast. Just what effect the Allegheny mountains will have cannot be stated at the moment, but a further bulletin will be issued by noon today.

"Shipping interests on Lake Erie and Lake Ontario should take precautions against the possible occurrence of winds of 40 to 70 miles per hour."

It is small wonder that "bulletin" did not really spark much reaction. The language is low-key, official, quite proper, concerned about the "considerable apprehension" that news stories might create. If that bulletin were read on the air, *verbatim*, as it almost certainly was, it is not too surprising that the average listener seems to have given it scant attention.

The second official bulletin around noon Friday was released only after a telephone conversation with the Central Analysis Office, which confirmed the previous prognosis. It read: "Hurricane Hazel moved inland just East of Myrtle Beach, South Carolina, at 9:15 Eastern. At 11:30 it was centred 30 miles West of Wilmington, North Carolina, and moving Northward with a speed of 30 miles per hour.

"The hurricane is expected to continue on its Northerly course, reaching the Eastern end of Lake Ontario about midnight tonight. In crossing the Allegheny mountains the hurricane will decrease markedly in intensity with winds not expected to exceed 50 miles per hour on the open water of Lake Ontario."

Again the same low-key language, much more likely to soothe listeners than to alarm them. Low-keyed language or not, after that bulletin, Fred Turnbull was sought for radio interviews. Contrary to existing government policies, he thought the situation extraordinary enough to go ahead and give interviews, doing several in the course of the day, and two more in the evening between 9:30 and midnight.

At 9:30 Friday night, the following synopsis and forecast was released:

Official Forecasts issued by the Dominion Public Weather Office in Toronto at 9:30 p.m. EST, Friday, October 15, 1954.

Synopsis:

Hurricane Hazel, which moved in on the North Carolina Coast Friday morning, continued to move northward and to accelerate during the day, and by 9:00 p.m. was centred between Buffalo and Rochester.

The intensity of this storm has decreased to the point where it should no longer be classified as a hurricane. This weakening storm will continue northward, passing just east of Toronto before midnight. The main rainfall associated with it should end shortly thereafter, with occasional light rain occurring throughout the night. Winds will increase slightly to 45 to 50 MPH until midnight, then slowly decrease throughout the remainder of the night.

Lake Ontario and Niagara Regions
Toronto and Hamilton Cities:
Rain tonight. Cloudy with occasional showers Saturday. Little change in temperature. Winds north 40 to 50 this evening decreasing overnight to northwest 30 Saturday. Low tonight and high Saturday at Toronto, St. Catharines, and Hamilton, 45 and 55. Outlook for Sunday cloudy and cool.

There, clearly, is the explanation for the dispute about whether Toronto was properly warned. Many people who listened to that broadcast simply did not hear any reference to a hurricane, or heard it in terms they did not understand. The measured tones of the announcer, going on to talk about the outlook for Sunday, did not spell any risk or danger to them. Whipper Billy Watson, for example, went out fishing, not exactly an activity one plans in the face of a hurricane. Gordon Sinclair, who has one of the keenest instincts for a story, was getting ready to go to New York; with his legendary memory, he can relate stories about the hurricane after it happened, but remembers no particular forewarning.

Some firms did send people home early, but they were exceptions rather than the rule. G. A. Burton remembers hearing hurricane warnings, and heeding them, not only by cancelling out on a commitment to a reception at the Lambton Golf Club, but by making preparations at home. He set out candles and filled bathtubs with water in case of power and water-supply failure or fire. Ken Dryden, then a small boy in Etobicoke dreaming small boys' dreams about being an NHL goalie, was impressed by how seriously his parents took the warning, establishing emergency procedures in case their household was affected.

But in the main, people went on about their business. Robert N. Brown was passing the old Long Branch racetrack about 4:00 and was surprised and disgusted to see the horses being whipped around the hopelessly waterlogged track, with the mud flying every which way. Business as usual. Marilyn Simser (then Marilyn McLean) was cheering on her school football team that afternoon. The continuous rain was just a nuisance, until it caused the game to be called off at half-time. Barry Tobe was refereeing another high-school football game, but decided to call the game off when the ball "kept floating off the field".

George Ennis and his wife decided it was a good afternoon to watch a movie. After the show, they got up to leave about 6:30. "As soon as we entered the lobby we began to suspect that this was no ordinary rain storm, as the lady selling tickets was no longer in the booth. She had had to seek shelter in the lobby as the rain was just pouring into the ticket booth."

Others planned trips. Peg MacMurray had been displaying books in Buffalo, and saw no reason why she should not drive home that evening.

Barrie L. Ralph (now an Anglican minister) was a

proud fifteen-year-old "completing the first evening of the first day of my first part-time job at Fridham's Grocery store". He had difficulty walking home because of the strong wind and heavy rain and his journey was not improved by a flying garbage-tin lid which struck him on the head – without "serious damage to either the lid or my head". Less amusingly, when Carole Tonner (aged ten) and her younger sister went off to meet their Dad's streetcar, they started to play in the gutter at Lonsdale and Spadina; the little girl was swept off her feet and carried against the grate that guarded the entrance to the sewer. That grate, and the men who pulled her out, saved her life.

Life went on. At first the rain was an inconvenience, causing traffic jams as people spent hours trying to get home from work, or away for the weekend, or off to important family events. Helen and Mervin Grant were married that Friday evening at 7:30 p.m. "I had said to Helen a few days before, 'Don't be late on Friday.' Helen said, 'Don't worry. I'll be there come hell or high water.' She was late too!"

Others attended wedding rehearsals, visited hospitals, played poker, prepared, like Mrs. Esther Schwartz's family, to celebrate the Jewish Sabbath eighteen minutes before sundown, or simply visited friends. In short, people were undeterred by the wet weather from doing the thousand and one things people do on Friday nights.

Clearly, the dangers threatened by the weather were not conveyed successfully to the people of Toronto. Later, Fred Turnbull, of the Weather Office, tried to discover why. The last paragraphs of his Hurricane Hazel report read:

"I am sure many since the major disaster of last Friday have asked, 'Why did it happen?' There no doubt are many, too, like myself, who have, in attempting to answer that question, at least to ourselves, in private soul-searching, asked, 'What could I have done which might have prevented the tragedy?'

"From a meteorological standpoint, it seems to me that every possible step was taken and taken in adequate time. It may be argued that we did not sufficiently stress the amount of rain, but even if we had been able to forecast even Malton's 5.3 inches of rain in terms of definite figures expressed in inches, I wonder how many, if any, would have interpreted a five-inch rainfall as a disastrous amount. Certainly I was fully aware that rainfall totals were likely to exceed the all-time record of four inches, but I definitely did not have sufficient knowledge of the Humber watershed or sufficient imagination to interpret that amount of rain in terms of the tragic flood conditions."

Here certainly are the words of a man of conscience, expressing the almost universal anguish at human lives lost and wondering how the outcome might have been different.

In summary, it seems fair to say that for what was to come there was plenty of warning, but not in a form that most people understood. Weather reports predicted winds and heavy rains; when it has been raining for a week, there is nothing in such a message to suggest that screaming winds and pelting rains unlike anything you have ever seen lie ahead.

So as Hurricane Hazel approached, no civil-emergency body was alerted. In truth, none existed worthy of the name. By a strange quirk of fate, the one man who had tried to organize such a force had resigned in despair only the day before. He was Air Vice-Marshal T. A. Lawrence, a man who believed in a civil-defence unit of trained and well-equipped people who could respond to local emergencies. When the federal government in Ottawa and municipal authorities began squabbling about who would pay for sirens, Ottawa chose to recall the equipment because the municipalities refused to bear the cost of installation. For Air Vice-Marshal Lawrence, it was just too much. He tendered his resignation to Mayor Saunders. His resignation took effect the same day Hazel struck.

Toronto was without a civil-defence unit. There were about forty auxiliary policemen who had signed on for a new training plan, but they were not called upon as a group because they had absolutely no equipment. Detective William Koopman, who was in charge of police civil defence at the time, said, "I couldn't have given them a shovel." Volunteer fire brigades were still the order of the day in townships and boroughs. Overall, there was no concerted strategy of defence for dealing with a major emergency.

If the city of Toronto had been about to face a blizzard, or was threatened by a fourteen-inch snowfall, *that* would have been something understandable. The message would have been clear, and it would have been understood. Equipment geared to many snowfalls of the past would have been at the ready, along with the work crews to man it. Accustomed to winter hazards, people would have known what limitations the storm placed on them and would have behaved accordingly.

This was different. This was the unknown, the unfamiliar, the totally unexpected crisis. Hurricanes belonged in the tropics. Because the Toronto area had no remembered history of such onslaughts by nature, none was ever expected.

It all began fairly quietly. By mid-afternoon the steady rains were producing deep puddles in underpasses. In the traffic jams that resulted, new records were set as half-hour journeys home from work took two or even three hours. Even today, many people can recall exactly how long their trip home that evening took. But Toronto had seen heavy rains and temporary floods before, so few people thought anything of it. By 6:00 p.m., however, the rain had turned into a torrential downpour ("blowing sideways", many people recall) and as it continued, slowly the realization grew that this was something special.

In the hours that followed it became clear that this was indeed special. The warm, tropical air of Hazel was colliding with the cold front moving eastward across Canada, and the result was a catastrophic rainfall. Long before Hazel officially hit the north shore of Lake Ontario at 11:10 p.m. on Friday, October 15, the winds that were the hurricane's outriders had swooped upon the Ontario shore. Winds of fifty-five miles per hour, and gusts of seventy-two miles per hour and higher, drove the heaviest rains in Toronto's history.

Like some malevolent force, viciously alive, the winds propelled the rain with the force of bullets. The rain, which had increased in intensity all day long, lashed the earth, buildings, trees, everything beneath it, until the sheets of water were so dense it looked as if some giant rain barrel had suddenly been upended. Only the stream was continuous; the giant rain barrel simply didn't give out. People spoke of the rain afterward as a "wall of water".

At Malton airport 5.9 inches of rain fell in the twelve hours up till 1:30 a.m. In the twenty-four hours, including the height of the storm, 7.20 inches of rain was dumped on the city, almost double the record of 3.88 inches in twenty-four hours in 1897. But the greatest concentration of rainfall was centred around Brampton, which recorded eight inches within a 48-hour period. In the three hundred square miles of the Humber watershed area, nearly nine inches fell on October 15 and 16. Since one inch of rainfall drops 14.5 million gallons of water on a square mile of ground, the watershed was hit with some forty billion gallons during Hazel, about two hundred million tons of water.

Because rain had been falling steadily for days earlier, the land was already soaked and sodden, like a dripping sponge that cannot absorb another drop. Most of the torrential rain thus ran off the already saturated land and poured straight down the valleys that cut north and south at sporadic intervals across the face of greater Toronto. When the Highland Creek, Don River, Humber River, Etobicoke Creek, Credit River, and Sixteen Mile Creek all began to overflow, rampaging waters chewed at riverbanks and bridges. At every bridge and every bend in the rivers the waters began to take their toll. Every stream became a roaring torrent, ranging far beyond its banks, as the area tried to cope with the forty billion gallons that were Hazel's parting gift.

Those are the facts. But the true story of Hurricane Hazel is the story of the people who were caught up in it. The fragments of their stories will help us to build a picture of how it felt to live through Hurricane Hazel.

CHAPTER FIVE

A NIGHT TO REMEMBER

At first it was all partly an inconvenience, partly a joke. The heavy rain that was falling as people left their offices and headed home that evening caused horrendous traffic jams, but also produced a number of funny incidents that people still recall. Rushing back from Toronto Teachers' College to her home in Acton for the weekend, Ena Gibson was soaked to the skin before she got on the train at Union Station. Rather than sit in her wet clothes, she squeezed into spare clothes from the suitcase of her much smaller friend Irene. Almost bursting out of her borrowed clothes, she spent the trip trying to hide in a corner, wondering why the train was taking so long. She learned later that she had caught the last train to get out of Toronto that night.

Young Bob Stuart, displaying the determination that was to make him a major figure in Canadian publishing, doggedly continued to deliver papers on his *Star* paper route, returning home to change no fewer than three times to the mingled amusement and consternation of his parents. Lena Tuck remembers that on her *Star* route she had "one customer who was so angry with me because he had received a wet paper" – despite the fact that Lena had struggled through waist-deep water to make her deliveries.

In Lansing, Kenneth Cheetham thought nothing of the news stories about a hurricane, "dismissing them as just a means of increasing circulation in a slack period". He was not at all alarmed by the rain: "After supper I took my four-year-old son and two of his sisters for an adventurous excursion along Hollywood Avenue. We were stopped dead in our tracks about one block from home. A culvert under the street which normally transported a mere trickle of muddy water through a lush growth of weeds was now a white-capped torrent roaring over the parapet a couple of feet above sea level and completely impassable." They went home to read the Winnie the Pooh story in which Piglet becomes "Entirely Surrounded By Water".

Dr. Mark Boyes was driving home up Bathurst Street: "When I reached the corner of Bathurst Street and Lawrence Avenue the intersection was quite flooded and there was a lone lady standing at a bus stop – the water was well above her ankles. I stopped and offered her a ride, which she gladly accepted. She stated that she had just been to the hairdresser 'and look at me *now!*' I remarked that it was a very heavy rainstorm and she burst forth: 'This is no rainstorm; this is a hurricane!' I still could not believe that it could be anything so drastic, but she assured me that she had heard reports on the radio."

Vera Reed also hitched a ride home, but found herself desperately fending off the Sicilian driver's amorous advances by singing choruses from *Cavalleria Rusticana*, which induced him to join in "at the top of his voice" and to stop planting kisses all the way up her left arm. The gallantly offered ride home ended without incident.

Even later in the day, there were still a few people

who couldn't believe what was going on around them. Nancy Hubbert's husband, for example, wanted to make use of the car they had borrowed. "On the night of Hazel, my husband (who doesn't believe in weather reports) suggested it might be nice to go up to Willowdale and visit friends. We duly hired a local youngster to baby-sit, whose mother had a comment or two to make about our sanity, and off we went. In the general vicinity of the Golden Mile, my husband decided the driver's door was rattling rather alarmingly and probably was not tightly closed, so he opened it to give it a good slam. Immediately it was wrenched off its hinges and took off into space. Frantically aware of the fact that this was a borrowed car, he was out in a flash, chasing the door until it came to rest, leaning against a truck in the parking lot. What to do! It obviously had to be removed to a safe place, so forgetting that he is a rather short, slight man, he picked it up by its sides to try to get it back to the car. Of course, a tremendous gust came along at the worst possible moment and suddenly there was the father of my children sailing through the air, madly clutching the door as it carried him through space, and I was collapsed in helpless laughter unable to offer even a small measure of help.

"When he finally came to rest, miraculously still on his feet, he found himself just outside the local drug store – Tamblyn's, I think – which was the only place still open in the plaza, and he made his way inside where he explained his predicament to the clerk and asked if he might leave the car door there until another day. As there was nothing in her rule book to cover such exigencies she decided it would probably be O.K., these being unusual circumstances, so between the two of them they managed to wrestle the door inside and lean it up against a display case. We then slowly and carefully inched our way home again, to our rented house, and our children, and our not too surprised baby-sitter, in our car with one door – and didn't venture out again for two days."

Mrs. Betty Dewar was taking a bus home from work through the flooded streets. "Going through one gully the water came up onto the floor. After we reached higher ground the driver simply opened the door and let the water run out. We all found it very funny."

Random incidents like these may have been comical, but as the winds blew and the torrential rains poured down on the city, a far from comical pattern began to emerge.

In the newsroom of the Toronto *Globe and Mail*, City Editor Robert Turnbull was planning to get away from the paper early in the evening to drive his wife and daughters to Buffalo for the weekend. When a 7:00 p.m. police radio message reported that the Stoney Creek circle of the Queen Elizabeth Highway was under a foot of water and that traffic was being diverted (including poor Peg MacMurray on her routine trip home from Buffalo) his reaction was simply to delay the family drive until the following morning.

Then began the first of a long series of reports and calls from staff members, citizens, and ham-radio operators, all with extraordinary stories. And so began the controlled chaos of a City Room in the midst of a major breaking story. Every available reporter and photographer was called in and assigned one phase of what was developing into a story of unsuspected proportions. Reporters Clark Davey, Bruce West, Ralph Hyman, Alden Baker, David Spurgeon, Ken MacTaggart, Rod Goodman, Ralph Blackmore, Wilf List, and Lotta Dempsey, and photographers Harold Robinson, Harry McLorinan, and John Boyd, all set to work on one of the most memorable assignments of their careers, and one which was to produce – miraculously – the payment of a bonus.

It's March 1954 and these three young Torontonians are thrilled at the prospect of taking a ride on Toronto's spanking new subway.   *Photo: Toronto Star*

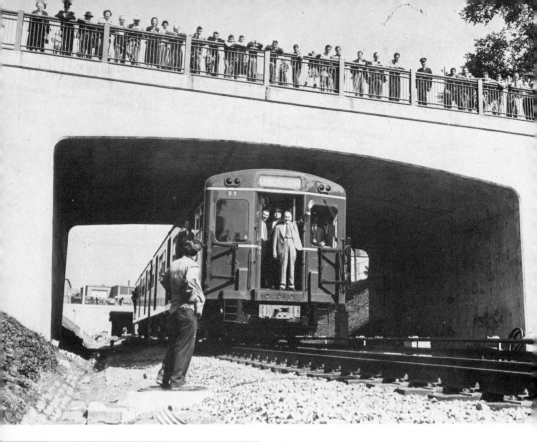

(Top) All the way along its first run, Toronto's subway attracted thrilled crowds. (Bottom) These crowds were nothing, however, compared to crowds attracted by Marilyn Bell in her triumphant swim across Lake Ontario in September 1954. *Photos: Toronto Star*

A month later Torontonians were still talking about Marilyn Bell's feat. Nobody paid much attention to the fact that a new-born hurricane, Hurricane Hazel, had devastated the Caribbean island of Haiti.

Even the Catholic church at Aux Cayes, the largest building in the town, proved to be no match for the hurricane. *Photos courtesy of Murdeen McIver*

(Top) The bride had promised to be there "come hell or high water", so Helen and Merv Grant were duly married on the evening of Friday, October 15. Here they prepare to drive away in Helen's sister's storm-spattered Chevrolet. Like thousands of other Ontarians, they had no idea of the extent of the disaster that was to hit the province. *Photo courtesy of Mr. and Mrs. M. G. Grant* (Bottom) And the rain continued to pour down. *Photo: Toronto Telegram, York University Archives*

As streams became rivers and city streets became waterways, it began to dawn on people that this was truly an emergency. *Photos: Toronto Telegram, York University Archives*

(Top) As the waters rose, many householders, like the Robinson family on the Eglinton Avenue Flats, were forced to spend an anxious night on the roof of their besieged home. *Photo: Toronto Telegram, York University Archives* (Bottom) Alex Nicholson's car ended up in the swollen Don River, and he spent five and a half hours clinging to a tree in the river before being rescued by a human chain of firemen. *Photo: Toronto Star*

(Top) In the space of a few hours these Torontonians were turned into refugees, glad to escape with their lives. *Photo: Toronto Star* (Bottom) Hundreds of children rescued from endangered houses spent the rest of that fateful night in hastily organized reception centres. *Photo: Toronto Telegram, York University Archives*

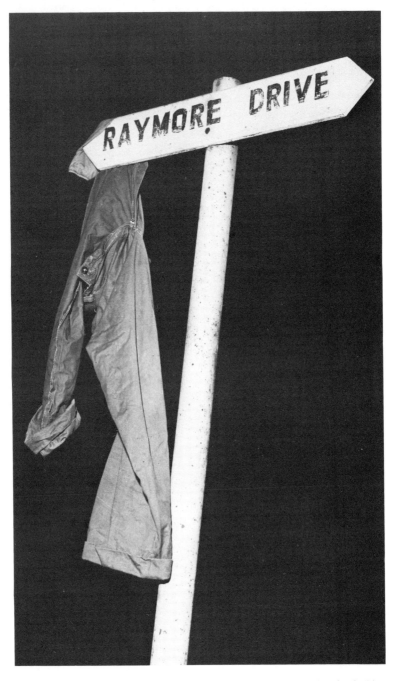

The street that disappeared.   *Photo: Toronto Telegram, York University Archives*

It was a scene repeated in the newsrooms of the *Star* and the *Telegram*. Hazel was not one story. It was a thousand stories to be told in the mosaic of hundreds of events and incidents over a broad Ontario landscape. The range of events made it difficult, even for those writing the news accounts, to gauge the magnitude of the story. For newspapermen, firemen, navy men, and scores of volunteers, the wildest, stormiest nightmare hours of Hurricane Hazel had begun.

As the rains fell and were funnelled into the streams and creeks that drain into the lake, the streams became raging rivers, and the bridges over them suddenly became death traps. Against the backdrop of those many bridges, a series of grim and deadly dramas were played out in the hours of darkness. Howling winds, the sinister roar of rivers on the rampage ("like a fast-moving freight train" John Ridpath remembers, the sound of the Humber River still in his ears), shrieks and cries for help, shouted instructions from would-be rescuers, all punctuated a black night made eerie with improvised light from torches and truck headlights.

Telephone linesman Gerald Elliot was among the first to encounter the flood hazard as he tried to drive home through the storm. He became trapped on a bridge across the Humber when the bank on both sides washed away, leaving the bridge standing with his car on it. Firemen from Aldershot and York Township threw him a hose, which he wrapped around his waist. When the firemen tried to pull him through the swift floodwaters to safety, the hose broke and Elliot was swept away by the river.

He remembers the pounding pressure of the water and his frantic efforts to grab for something, anything, to hang on to. He managed to catch the branch of a tree; his car pitched into the water, swirled crazily in the current, and came to rest against the same tree. For a few moments he was in the incongruous position of standing atop his car, frantically clutching the tree. When both the car and the tree were swept away in the current, Elliot was convinced his life was over.

Recounting the escape later to reporter Donald Goudy of the *Toronto Daily Star*, Elliot said, "Then by some miraculous stroke of luck, my hand felt another branch in the water. I grabbed and struggled until I could pull myself up close against that small willow tree."

For the next four hours Elliot was to cling to that branch, visibly growing weaker, while firemen and police trained their lights on him and several hundred people watched rescue attempts fail repeatedly. A 65-foot aerial ladder from a fire truck didn't come anywhere close. Fired lines didn't fare any better, blown off course by the howling gale. Several boats were launched and capsized. A helicopter was summoned, but the darkness made it impossible for it to effect a rescue. Finally, it was a brave man named Max Hurley who successfully navigated a small boat through the current, choosing a sheltered path through a grove of broken and bent trees. Using fallen branches for leverage to pull himself slowly, cautiously upstream, he reached Elliot, put out a hand to the shivering and shaken man, and helped him clamber aboard. The watching crowd shouted victoriously, "He's got him. . . . he's got him!"

Elliot was rushed to St. Joseph's Hospital, suffering from exposure, shock, and jaws made sore from the constant chattering of his teeth from the cold.

While the Humber Valley was to be the scene of most of the disasters in the city that night, the Don Valley in the east did not escape untouched. Jack Biggs, twenty-seven, was in his car when it was washed into the Don River from the Pottery Road bridge. Again, great good fortune and determination enabled him to grab a small tree, and cling to it until he was rescued. Trevor Clark and Alex Nicholson were other motorists who ended up in the Don and were fortunate enough to be rescued.

Jim McArthur and his family had a very different experience; their home was in the valley. "The McArthur family lived in the Don Valley north of the Prince Edward Viaduct for over fifty years. My father and his father before him had kept an apiary of over one hundred colonies at the junction of Park Drive Reservation and the CNR main line. Now our homestead has been replaced by the interchange to Castle Frank on the Bayview Extension.

"This homestead was a wild and beautiful oasis in the middle of the city as we grew up. Our homes were located on an elevated plot of land which became an island each spring. We were accustomed to the annual spring flooding of the Don River and would just wait it out. That Friday in October was something else again.

"The high winds and heavy downpours were very unusual, as was the dead calm that followed. We experienced the usual flooding in the evening, with the water running down the road in front of our homes, but paid little heed to it. As we patrolled around our island some time around 11:00 or 11:30 that evening, we became aware of a sudden rush of water, as though a dam had given way. Suddenly the water began to rise in the driveways between the houses. Then it poured into the window wells and under all the doors.

"There were four families living on that island. My neighbour, Jerry, and I rounded everyone up. We were able to make our way to the high ground (the hills of Rosedale) through the back of our property by wading waist deep in water for about two hundred yards. It was terribly cold and we had no lights. We had phoned out to our friends. They met us at the top of the hill and gave us shelter for the night.

"My uncle Bill, who had lived in the valley all his life, refused to leave with us. He sat on the stairs to the second floor of his house and watched the water creep up, one step at a time. He tells of watching everything turn upside down. The lights began to pop and finally all went dark as the water shorted out the fuse box. The water eventually rose five and a half feet on the first floor and ruined everything.

"Wondering if the houses would still remain, I returned very early the next morning. Chaos was everywhere. My father's bee hives had floated away and were piled up helter-skelter at the bottom of the field. The bees, of course, had drowned. Trees, lumber, doors, tires, and drums were stacked up in the trees surrounding the houses. Our cars were sitting where we had left them but were full of water. I really wasn't aware of the total effect that Hazel wrought on the whole city as I was too busy for the next two weeks cleaning up the mess. I did hear a story of one man who lived further up the Don at Pottery Road who spent the night up in a tree until rescued the following morning.

"Bridges were moved off their pilings and floated downstream until they came to the Prince Edward Viaduct. There they jammed and the result was one of the biggest piles of wood, trees, garbage, etc., one has ever seen. Months afterwards work crews were busy burning the debris – and looking for bodies. None were found, as far as I know. No one drowned in the Don Valley as some did on the Humber.

"The worst experience we suffered came after the storm. The vilest individuals who prey on the misfortunes of others came scavenging around our homes hoping to pilfer items and run off with them. I drove a number away with the threat of a rifle, and I think I could have used it as I felt so depressed."

As the evening wore on, many families were involved in a nightmare of uncertainty. Max de Godart du Planty's wife, for example, was expecting their second child any day. As the couple sat through the hurricane they were painfully aware that their house was surrounded by many large trees. In the violence of the storm, a great pine tree snapped off six feet above ground and fell with such force that one branch was driven five feet into the earth. Next, a giant acacia tree fell, with a crash that shook the house. Its fall tore down power and phone lines, and for the next five or six hours they sat in the dark, listening to the crash of other falling trees, as the substantially built house trembled and reverberated in the force of hurricane winds.

By 2:00 a.m., when things seemed quieter, a dazed and anxious father-to-be was able to venture outside and take stock of the damage by the light of a flashlight. No fewer than ten trees, many of which could have hit the house, were down, fallen and twisted in all directions, blocking both the driveway to the house and the adjoining road to town. The lawn was littered with debris. On a further part of the property, a wood of poplars looked as though it had been mown like grass. Max de Godart du Planty says it speaks volumes for the steadiness of his wife's nerves that one week later their second baby arrived, perfectly sound. Today there is not a single tree within striking distance of their house.

Bruce and Peggy Randall had a terrifying experience with a falling tree. It knocked down a hydro pole at the foot of their garden, and for the rest of the night they and their daughters watched "bolts of electricity flashing across the lawn in the dark." In the morning they were all rescued safely from their house, which had been completely surrounded by these live wires."

Joan Prezio's family lived on a section of land where Scarlett Road crossed the Humber River. For over forty years her great-grandparents ran an ice cream parlour at that location. During the hurricane her old grandad decided if he had lived by the river most of his life, he'd die by it. But his sons literally carried him from the house. In the hours that followed, the water rose up to the eavestroughs.

It was days before the family were able to go back to face the incredible clean-up job. The home had to be shovelled out. Freezers full of spoiled and rotting food, combined with dirty floodwaters, gave off a stench that was nauseating. It was a heartbreaking task. The return to the house was not long-lived, for it was one of the homes expropriated for safety reasons. In later years, Joan Prezio would show her own children a park area, where once their ancestors had lived and had survived a hurricane called "Hazel".

Mrs. Dianne Lockhart (then Dianne Cornelius) has the clear memories of a twelve-year-old of that October night. She remembers coming home to their corner house at Gilhaven and Raymore Drive with a school friend who was to stay overnight. The youngsters amused themselves laughing and chatting over school books, while Dianne's mother was busy sewing. Mrs. Cornelius was making a dress for the newly arrived infant Nancy, a little niece who lived in Edmonton.

When the hydro began going off and on, it signalled the first signs of trouble. Reg Whibley, a neighbour, came to tell Dianne's father, Frank Cornelius, the river was rising. Cornelius asked Georgie Bridger to go around to Raymore Drive and warn people they might have to get out.

Frank Cornelius, his brother-in-law Chet Swales, Reg Whibley, and Bridger then began making rescue forays with a fourteen-foot cedar-strip boat. Working in swiftly rising waters, sometimes jumping into the water to pull and push the boat around obstacles, they were able to bring some residents to safety.

A father and son by the name of McGarvey were the last to dash to safety across a bridge that burst from its moorings. Only then did they discover that the rest of the McGarvey family – the mother, a son, and a daughter – were trapped in their home. McGarvey, desperate to reach them, had to be physically restrained by Cornelius, who finally knocked him down and tied him to a tree. From this position McGarvey watched as his house, with the family inside, was torn off its foundations and swept away, a grim shape that bobbed and disappeared into blackness.

The boat rescue operations Cornelius and the others were involved in were extremely hazardous, and Cornelius himself had a nightmare ride in the murky waters of the Humber. While trying to help someone into the boat, he fell into the river and was instantly swept away. In the end he managed to struggle ashore a quarter of a mile downstream, but by that time the woman he was rescuing had reported Frank Cornelius missing.

Although his immediate family did not know of this report, Frank's brother Desmond, in Edmonton, inquired and received the "missing" report from the Red Cross there. Desmond Cornelius, his wife Gwen, their three young sons, and their brand-new daughter Nancy promptly piled into the family car and set out for Toronto, to come to the aid of Frank's family. They were in a severe car accident; the baby Nancy was killed and the parents were badly injured; only the three little boys escaped unharmed. The long arm of Hazel had reached out across a thousand miles.

Nearer home, Mrs. G. F. Parrott found herself tend-ing a sick child – the little boy's temperature was 104 degrees – while the doctor was unable to reach him. "He had to give up and phone me. As I sat by my son, doing what the doctor said to do, he held the line and I kept going back to the phone to report my progress."

Diane Sonego also encountered help when she badly needed it: "I loved the TTC after Hurricane Hazel. I was just a young girl sitting in the bus terminal at Glen Echo. The storm was raging and I was crying; it was after midnight. The rain was coming down so hard, and it was so dark. A Wilson bus pulled into the station and the driver said, 'Never mind, little girl, I'll get you home.'

"Wilson Avenue was a river. We only knew where it was because of the telephone poles. In places the driver had to leave the road and drive on the lawns. . . . He got me home about 1:30 a.m."

There were many other kind deeds done that night. Joan Price's grandmother, "a rather thin, strong-willed old lady", lived down on the flats near the Humber River. "Granny was wakened that night by a man knocking at her door. Knowing that she lived alone, he had come down the hill when he noticed the water rising. But Granny was not to be rushed out of a house in which the water was up to her knees. No matter how this man pleaded and argued, Granny had to get fully dressed, corset and all, before she would leave the house. By the time the man helped, pushed and pulled Granny up the hill, her house had been washed away."

Another Good Samaritan came to the rescue of Ethel Forrester, then living with her fourteen-year-old son in a trailer camp in Long Branch: "We had retired for the night and were both asleep when we were awakened by a knock at the door. I opened it to find a man in oilskins with a flashlight, standing in a large puddle of water in the pouring rain. He said, 'Ma'am, there is a terrible storm and the creek is expected to flood. You should get out now while you have the chance.' I thanked him for the information, closed the door with thoughts that the best place to spend the night in a storm was inside my cosy warm trailer, then went back to bed.

"After about half an hour there was another knock on the door. This time the water was ankle deep and the man was more persistent in his demands that we get out and on to high ground. The rain and howling wind convinced me he was right. He told me to get a few things together and he would be back for us. We put on boots and a coat over our pyjamas and stood at the door watching the rising water. A man with a small pick-up truck came and asked if we needed help. He offered to take us to the Lakeshore Road. As we got into the front seat I could see the water was now up to his hub caps. He had a small dog that he gave to my son to hold and told us how he *just happened* to be driving by the trailer camp, saw the flood, and thought someone might need help.

"He tried to drive to the Lakeshore Road but halfway there realized the water was too deep, so he turned back to try and get to the railroad tracks that were on high ground north of the trailer camp. By this time the water was so deep it was starting to come in the doors. We then knew we should get out before we were trapped inside the truck. With difficulty we opened the doors, and stepped into ice-cold water swirling up to our waist. He carried me; I carried his little dog; and son John half swam and half waded to the railroad embankment. Here on dry ground he left us, and took his little dog back into the swirling water to rescue someone else.

"We climbed up the bank where many other people were standing in the bitter-cold wind, mostly in night clothes. One man offered me a drink of his bottle of spirits which I took. We then decided to walk to a road that was still high and dry. This would take us to Lakeshore Road. Here we managed to hitch a ride to a friend's house."

As the rising waters drove people out of their houses, emergency shelters had to be provided for them; supplies to fight the storm were badly needed. One of the gallant people who helped at the height of the hurricane was William Solomon, a druggist. He was called upon by the Red Cross to help, and his panel truck was soon at work delivering things like rubber boots and ropes where they were needed. He took them to a church on the outskirts of the flooded area: "I'll never forget the sight. Hundreds of people, babies crying, everyone huddled together, people looking for friends and relatives, a woman in shock, saying over and over again, 'The whole street disappeared.' "

Mr. Solomon was soon involved delivering bread – provided free by the President of Christie's – to a hospital that was stranded and out of food. Back at the Red Cross Headquarters in Islington he learned of the death of several good friends: "I just sat down on the floor, completely exhausted, and wept, unashamedly."

Without pausing for sleep he went out to open the drug store, where he found that his phones were the only ones in the area still working. Soon he was fielding calls from as far away as San Francisco and Vancouver, inquiring about the safety of people in his neighbourhood. The lines of local families anxious to make calls grew until there was a queue of about thirty people. "I called the Bell Telephone and described the situation. A truck with ten pay phones arrived that afternoon and people were allowed to use these pay phones free until service was restored."

Several people who were unaffected by the hurricane

(apart from suffering the flooded basements that affected practically every household in the city) commented on the eerie feeling in the air. After an evening at the 'Y', Ken Steele set off for home: "I would say that it must have been around 10:30 or 11:00 that night that while walking home, alone, on Dovercourt Road, I noticed something strange in the air. It was the eeriest feeling that I have ever experienced and it has not happened to me since. It was extremely quiet, the weather mild. There was a great stillness in the air – nothing seemed to move around me. I remember looking up at the trees – not a leaf trembled. No automobiles, even, that I was aware of. (Of course, traffic was much lighter in those days.) I felt I was in a vacuum. Upon arriving home, I thought no more of it.

"The next morning (Saturday) another surprise was in store for me. When I awakened and turned on the bed-side radio, I honestly thought I was listening to an Orson Welles play – the announcer was talking very excitedly about houses being swept down the river with people clinging to the rooftops, pandemonium everywhere. It was only when he mentioned the Humber River that I came to my full senses and realized it was for real."

Kenneth Cheetham, his task of reading *Winnie the Pooh* long completed, noticed that the hurricane-force winds from the south had died, presumably as the eye passed over. Around midnight he ventured out to find that the winds were now gusting from the north.

His reflections on the hurricane reflect the general surprise at the number of deaths by drowning: "I'd always thought of a flood as something that rose gradually, like the tide, from which you could always escape when it reached an unacceptable height, albeit with sacrifice of material possessions. But Hazel was not a tide, but a tidal wave, sweeping unprepared and unsuspecting people to their deaths in a matter of moments. Maybe most major disasters happen like this – they sneak up on you unexpectedly."

OUTSIDE THE CITY

In the course of Hurricane Hazel's unexpected visit to Canada, Toronto was the area hardest hit. Yet much of the rest of Ontario was severely affected as Hazel dealt death and destruction over a wide swath of the province before blowing out over James Bay.

One of the first towns to suffer was Niagara-on-the-Lake, the scenic little town that perches just across the Niagara gorge from the United States. Grant Knox was a sixteen-year-old there, very conscious of the fact that, if be behaved himself, the family car (a 1952 Oldsmobile) was available for local jaunts: "When the Hurricane hit Niagara I was driving in our long driveway to the house. The weather irregularities lasted for less than ten minutes. Just as I parked the car at the end of the driveway it literally shook like hell. It rolled from side to side while I was sitting parked in it, and I thought for sure it would roll over on the roof. All I could think of was I was going to catch hell from my father for having an accident in the driveway. He would never actually believe the truth in this occurrence. . . . "

As the storm swept north through the province, it caused washouts, power failures, downed hydro wires,

disrupted transportation, traffic accidents, flooded highways, and washed-out bridges. These in turn produced
scenes of disruption which grew grimmer as the night
wore on. The battering rain and gale-force winds seemed
interminable. In Meaford, the shoreline community saw
ships and boats sunk in the harbour, while waves burst
over breakwaters to roll in over the waterfront streets.

Captain D. MacRitchie was aboard a Great Lakes
freighter en route from Rochester, New York, to Toronto.
He recalls that it took five and one-half hours to run
what normally would have taken half that time. With
wind and rain making it impossible to see anything, he
relied on radar to take them across the Toronto bay and
up the ship channel to Weaver's dock, where the ship lay
at dock for eighteen hours waiting for the seas to abate.
The yard of the coal dock had from one to three feet of
water, which was spilling over the edge of the dock like a
stream of black soup.

Leo Fitzgerald, who was unloading a Great Lakes
freighter at Point Anne, near Belleville, remembers wind
so strong it was impossible to stand on deck. If you held
onto the ship's railing, you were blown straight out like
clothes on a line.

For CPR Engineer Herbert Stitt aboard Engine No.
1259 out of Toronto for Peterborough at 6:00 p.m. that
Friday evening, it was the start of a run that would have
seemed implausible, even in a movie. As the train, with
its baggage car and three full passenger coaches, crossed
the Rouge River bridge, the water was only a foot below
the deck of the bridge. (Less than two hours later the
bridge was gone.) Two miles down the track, a culvert
weakened by the rain sagged so drastically that some of
the alarmed passengers began to scream. The engine
broke away from the train and the emergency brakes
abruptly halted both train and engine. The flagman who

went to attend to the recoupling fell into the culvert, sustaining an injury to his knee that would lay him up for several weeks. The baggage man had great difficulty getting the flagman back aboard the train, and the train recoupled.

Pulling into the passing track near Locust Hill, Engineer Stitt (an old front-line soldier in the First World War) instinctively ducked his head when he saw several corrugated sheets of metal roofing flying around like sheets of newspaper. A large black mass sailed past the cab and landed with a crash on the back of the tender. Halting the train again, Engineer Stitt and his fireman, William Munroe, tried unsuccessfully to dislodge what proved to be the larger portion of a coal-shed roof. There was nothing to do but uncouple the engine again, pull it ahead, and allow the roof to fall to the ground, where several section men could remove it.

On the balance of the journey to Peterborough the train was stopped five more times and section men were called out to saw trees and remove them from the tracks. All this time Engineer Stitt had the small front window open in an effort to see, and consequently was soaked to the hide. Eight hours after leaving Toronto the train arrived in Peterborough to the thanks of weary and unnerved passengers.

Engineer Stitt, now eighty-two, says, "As a front-line soldier in the 1914-18 war, I thought I would never see so much rain, but that night sure changed my mind."

A CNR passenger train struck a washout at Markham and the locomotive and express car toppled off the tracks to lie on their side in the mud. Mrs. Fred Nobbs remembers the incident well, since it happened just behind the Nobbs barn. Nobody was hurt, and Mrs. Nobbs made coffee "by the gallon" for the survivors, who spent the night in the train or in nearby farms.

Ernie Bustard, a naval architect, discovered war-time reminders in the course of an apparently routine trip by car from Toronto to Collingwood. After hours of detours to avoid blocked roads, he and the wife of a Collingwood friend found themselves stuck at "the BA gas station just fourteen miles south of Barrie. Inside, the scene was like a downtown bar at lunchtime. By now it was late evening and the staff were doing a great job of providing sandwiches for everyone. There was no shortage of bread as two bread trucks were among those waiting out the storm, and the drivers brought in whatever the staff required. The whole atmosphere was one of camaraderie, almost like that of an air-raid shelter during wartime." Vince Farr, a *Star* reporter, was stranded in the same spot, which, in his words "resembled a miniature Grand Central Station as 350 persons were marooned from 9 o'clock on."

About 5:00 a.m. Ernie Bustard and his companion were able to get north to Barrie and, after many detours, home to Collingwood sixteen hours after they had set out from Toronto.

Barrie itself was especially badly affected, with a thirty-foot-wide river covering one of the streets to the depth of almost a foot. Areas beside water of any sort – no matter how peaceable or safe they normally seemed – were very much in danger at Barrie that night. By midnight, for example, the Saugeen River was seven and one-half feet above its normal level, and rising ten inches an hour. Meanwhile, waves estimated at an unbelievable fifteen feet crashed through the Richardson Boat Works, washing away a 26-foot sailboat, which was never seen again.

I. S. McClure, who was with the Municipal Detachment of the Ontario Provincial Police at Barrie, spent the late afternoon of October 15 on point duty at an intersection known as "Five Points". Because of the heavy rain he was wearing rubber boots, not part of dress issue, and a raincoat long enough to cover them. At 7:00 when he returned to the office he was, none the less, soaked through. He was assigned desk duty answering phones, no doubt to give him a chance to dry.

He recalls, "Our office had three lines and they rang continuously until about 9:00 p.m. when water must have gotten into them and they went dead. The calls were mostly from people whose houses were surrounded by water and who were requesting assistance. All I could do was advise them to remain inside until the water subsided. I had several calls from people who wanted to know if this was the end of the world – something which I was not in a position to answer.

"After the phones went out of order, I was sent on patrol. The amount of water visible was beyond comprehension. At the intersection of Collier and Clapperton streets, the flowing water swept a woman and child off their feet and carried them down the Clapperton Street hill. They were rescued by employees of Deluxe Taxi and taken into their office.

"The water in Kempenfeldt Bay [part of Lake Simcoe] had risen sufficiently to cover parts of Simcoe Street along the CNR railway tracks. At the foot of Mary Street, where it meets Simcoe Street, the water had undermined the railway tracks deep enough that a car would have been able to go under the tracks, which were four lines wide.

"At the highest point at the top of Bayfield Street Hill, I had a flat tire on the cruiser and subsequently received another soaking. The depth of water at the top of the hill on the pavement was about four inches. This to me was an unbelievable sight, because it was the very highest point of land in the area. It caused me to wonder where all the water could be coming from.

"A large storm sewer crosses Peel Street, but it was able to carry only a minute quantity of the water, so the extra ran above ground. It carried with it the front steps of a house on Peel Street, for almost a city block. When I refer to front steps, it was a solid block of cement, about six feet across and five feet high, with steps moulded into one side. The strangest thing about it was that it was left in an upright position with the railing still attached. Since the flood, now so many years ago, a large apartment building has been built on the very lowest part of the gully at Peel Street. When I pass it, I wonder what will become of it, should the Lord decide to send another flood."

Rhoda Duke was living on a farm in Muskoka when Hurricane Hazel struck. Their farm had a good barn with a rock stable. When the storm hit the barn, it lifted it up off the stable and set it down again on the ground near by. In the now roofless stable stalls stood the Dukes' five cows, unhurt, and apparently undisturbed.

The cows on Ruth and Gilbert Agar's Kleinburg farm were less composed. When Gilbert went out in the storm on horseback to bring them in for milking they refused to cross the floating bridge across a badly flooded culvert. When they scattered in frightened disarray there was nothing for Gilbert Agar to do but send the horse back and struggle home alone, to find his wife in the barn with water a foot deep charging through. Marian Armstrong remembers that the cows on her Unionville farm "seemed possessed. . . . They went round and round the house, meeting one another, turning at times to join a group and then in turn reversing the order. . . . By morning that green pasture field looked like a field of mud. They must have run all night."

Farmers all over seemed to have similar experiences; when Robin Reil, a school teacher in Perth, asked his

Grade 8 science classes to discover what Hurricane Hazel had done to their area, all of their parents and grandparents recalled many incidences of barns blowing down and farm equipment and livestock being harmed in the Perth and Arnprior areas of the Ottawa Valley. In Ottawa itself, a young 22-year-old man was electrocuted by fallen power lines.

Farther south, near Peterborough, a major tragedy was narrowly averted simply because Hazel did not come a week earlier or a week later. Roberta Beamish explains: "In 1954, I was a young rural school teacher in the community of South Dummer, about fifteen miles east of Peterborough. In order to raise money to take the children on a trip at the end of the year – we had taken the Thousand Islands tour the year before – we held dances in the school every other Friday night. On the late afternoon of the dance, the boys would pile the desks along the wall, sweep the floor – sometimes even scrub and wax it – and the girls would make sandwiches and set out things for the tea or coffee. Most of the kids would be there with their parents that evening to help serve and to enjoy the community get-together.

"Hazel arrived sometime during the night on Friday, October 15, and when it left, the brick gable end of the school was lying on the dance floor, amid plaster and splintered two-by-fours. Fortunately, Hazel's visit occurred on an in-between Friday. Had she arrived unannounced the week before or a week later, several of us would certainly have been killed or severely injured."

It was not an ideal night to be travelling about the province. In his book *Press Gang,* James B. Lamb tells how a group of youngsters who were carriers for the *Orillia Packet and Times* were sent on a prize-winners' trip to Toronto at the paper's expense. So far so good. Unfortunately the trip, to watch a hockey game at Maple Leaf

Gardens, was on October 15. As the editor of the paper, Jim Lamb was in anguished suspense: "Like half a hundred anxious parents, we spent a wakeful night trying to learn what had become of them on that terrible occasion, but we needn't have worried. After the hockey game, which many of them spent at the refreshment booths under the stands, they enjoyed an uproarious night at their downtown hotel, dropping water bombs made of paper towelling down the air shafts."

Alph McGlynn, driving a chartered busload of less exuberant people from Preston to Toronto to attend a play at the Exhibition grounds, remembers wind and rain so intense that the rain was driven through the bus windows, and passengers used their umbrellas to keep the rain off them *inside* the bus.

Things were, if anything, even worse for those travelling by train. Mrs. Bertha Whittaker, for instance, was returning home to Southampton, Ontario, that night. When she changed trains in London, the water was running over the curb. "It continued to rain throughout the trip. When within a few hundred yards of the Southampton Depot, the train toppled over on its side. The windows smashed. I was sitting there with the water running around me and blood running down my face. I sat there and prayed, for an indefinite time, until the firemen rescued me."

Mrs. Whittaker was taken to Saugeen Memorial Hospital suffering from shock, bruises, and a separated shoulder. The engineer, Gordon McCallum of Palmerston, and fireman, Stewart Nicholson of nearby Southampton, were trapped in the cab, and both died of injuries sustained when the train's boiler burst. George A. Wright recalls: "The whole town mourned the victims of Hurricane Hazel . . . everyone knew these two men."

Edna Craven and her husband Gerry had evening

plans and with their niece (their baby-sitter) and young son aboard they set out from Toronto for Orangeville at 5:00. They had not bargained for the storm and the traffic tangles it created; by seven they were only at Bloor Street. By the time they reached St. Clair, they had begun to realize this was no ordinary storm, since the force of water had lifted manhole covers, and geysers of water were shooting four feet into the air. A variety of attempts at many different roads eventually led the Cravens to the Queen Elizabeth Highway. After hours of nerve-wracking, exhausting driving, under the most hazardous conditions, they turned north, hoping to get away from the lake and the swollen streams rushing into it. Their new plan was to make it to Brampton and find a hotel. Safety and shelter were what they sought.

By now, water was so deep on the roadways, it was trickling across the floor of the car. They came to a dip in the road ahead filled with abandoned cars. There was no way to go ahead. They dared not turn back. It was by now one in the morning.

Leaving her husband Gerry to cope with the car and occupants, Edna Craven set out in the storm to seek shelter for them. At the first house it was obvious the desperate young woman baby-sitting there was in no position to help anyone. At the next house the couple were more than willing to do anything they could, but their own situation was one of crisis. They had just received word that the flat roof of their factory was about to cave in under the weight of water, and they were desperately trying to get workmen to come and help. When Mrs. Craven said she would like to try to reach the Charteris family, whom they knew, the woman of the house told her the Charteris family was out of town but said she wouldn't want to turn the Cravens away – she would make some arrangement. She was sure her son could put them up for the night.

Some moments later, a car arrived at the door and, after collecting Mr. Craven, Doris, and young Howard, took them all to another house, where they found themselves the guests of a young Crown attorney named Bill Davis and his wife. The Davises' hospitality was warm and thoughtful, as though there were nothing unusual about four total strangers arriving wet and bedraggled as house guests in the middle of the night. Nowadays, when the Cravens run into Premier William Davis, Mrs. Craven delights in telling him they still remember that night – every time they vote in a provincial election.

At the Foymount radar station, located at the highest point in southern Ontario, eighty miles west of Ottawa and eighty miles north of Belleville, Donald H. Washington was duty controller along with a crew of six or eight radar operators and technicians on October 15. They provided surveillance of air traffic, and could also observe and report on the movement of storm fronts. That night the radar echoes from Hazel obliterated the entire southwest quadrant of their radar scope to a range of 150 miles and beyond. As the storm grew near, the wind velocities increased from 50 to 60 and then to 80 miles per hour, with gusts to 115 miles per hour recorded on the anemograph logs.

The four-storey, windowless, structural steel building in which Donald Washington was working shuddered, shrieked, and shook. The 32-foot radar antenna atop the building was always protected by a neoprene-covered balloon structure; on this night it had to be inflated to five times its normal pressure to withstand the force of the wind. The radar did keep functioning, but the radio and telephone communications were knocked out. While the men felt they were in no immediate danger, they were concerned for families and friends in the area, especially when they found forty-five heavy drums full of oil scattered like ten-pins about the site. For Donald Washington, it was the most memorable of the many hundreds of graveyard shifts spent at radar stations in Canada.

For Jackson Glassford, a Beeton farmer, the night was to hold grim and terrible memories. Glassford and his son, Allan, spent four frantic hours trying vainly to rescue Mr. and Mrs. Otto Haugh and John Haugh (all of Egbert) and their friend Robert Edgar of Baxter from the top of their car, which had been swept off a bridge. Just before the Haughs' car was caught in the floodwaters, Ervin Joyce, twenty-two, had been swept to his death as he bravely tried to warn the Haughs away.

The four passengers managed to cling to their car, which remained afloat, while efforts were made to reach them in midstream and bring them to safety. Attempts to get a boat within rescue distance took considerable time. Even 175 feet of cable proved inadequate for the reach. With another 25 feet of cable attached, it looked as though the rescue were possible, if young Allan went into the water up to his neck, guiding the cable. Foot by foot the cable was paid out until the boat reached the marooned people. One, two, three, they entered the boat. Then, as the fourth person got into the boat, a wave hit it, turned it over, and all four were lost in the darkness.

East of Toronto, the Rouge River was in full spate, very different from the placid stretch of water Ted Ryan thought he knew: "Shortly after 10:00 that night the phone rang. It was my friend and neighbour, Fred Hunt. He asked me if he could borrow my auto-top boat which we used for duck hunting as he had gotten word at the corner store there were one or two families stranded in the lower Rouge River due to flooding.

"Fred was at the house in a few minutes to pick up the boat and said he was headed to the foot of Island Road, which was the logical place to commence operations. I

asked him to wait for me there until I got more appropriately dressed. When I was racing out the door, my wife,
who was eight months pregnant, said, 'Don't you be going down the river in that boat.' There was no way I was
going to miss out on this adventure as the Rouge area
was quite rural at this time and this sort of thing was one
of our pleasures. Of course, I had in mind that we would
serenely cruise down the river and, with some luck, possibly rescue a damsel in distress.

"When I arrived at the launching site, the scene was
much different from what I had imagined. There were a
few people gathered around one of the local fire trucks
and the firemen (volunteers) were playing search lights
down river, illuminating what appeared to be some cottages or houses in the distance. The wind was now a
high-pitched scream. There was no river; the whole valley was a raging torrent trying to discharge itself into
Lake Ontario, but was being partially dammed by the
Rouge River railway trestle at its mouth.

"My boat was sitting at the water's edge but Fred was
not there. When I asked regarding his whereabouts, they
said, 'Oh, he's gone down the river in another boat with
one of the firemen.' This made me angry to think that he
would go without me, as we had spent many hours in
boats together.

"Gil Read, the owner of the corner store, arrived on
the scene and I asked him if he would go with me. Gil
was a little reluctant – maybe he figured he had had
enough close calls in the tank corps during the war and
shouldn't press his luck. In any event I talked him into it
– and I may say here that I would not do it again, at least
not in a twelve-foot flat-end canoe.

"Well, with the help of the firemen, we got the boat
out into water deep enough to mount the motor. Gil got
in the front, myself in the back. Both of us are over six

feet in height, weighing over two hundred pounds, so you can see we had a fair load to start with. After a few cranks the motor caught and we slowly moved out to the main stream.

"That was the last time we had any positive control over the boat. I knew we were in trouble, and it would be just a matter of time before we would upset.

"All sorts of things were tumbling downstream with us – pieces of houses, furniture, and I can remember one huge uprooted tree thrashing around just to the right of our path. We went past it at the right time, otherwise we would have cracked like an egg shell.

"We were now running over people's front lawns, which were eight feet under us, and then we ran into a tree. (Although we didn't realize it at that moment, this tree saved our lives, and a few other lives, as we shall see.) I was able to hold onto a substantial branch of the tree which was at chest level. I don't know what caused it, but the boat started to sink beneath us, and then, in seconds, the current whipped it away into the darkness.

"My tree limb was strong and, needless to say, I was holding on for dear life. Gil was not so fortunate. All he could grab was a light branch that was already starting to give way. We were both stretched out horizontally in the silly current, and this is where long legs can come in handy. Gil made a desperate lunge and managed to get a hold of my ankles and crawl slowly over me and then up into a higher branch of the tree. There we both were, sitting in the tree like a couple of wet owls, not too proud of our seamanship.

"In the meantime, Fred Hunt and Howard Morgan, in a boat not much larger than ours, had evacuated two women and we could now see them coming down the river again to pick up two youths who were standing in the upper window about thirty feet from where we sat perched in their tree. We could not make ourselves heard above the howling wind and at that time no one knew what had happened to us.

"We watched them load up the two lads and a dog, and then nose their boat out to head upstream. About halfway between the house and our tree, what looked like a dog kennel came tossing and turning, hitting the nose of their boat, causing the current to force them right against our tree. We exchanged greetings, told our story, and chitchatted back and forth with all of us trying to figure out a solution to get their boat, which was broadside, nose upstream without capsizing it. Fred had handed a flashlight to me, with which I was making simulated Morse code signals upstream to make someone up there aware that we had problems.

"Moments later I happened to shine the light into their boat. Water was pouring over the back, and within thirty seconds we had six bodies in the tree. The boat disappeared with the dog and I never did find out if he survived. To my knowledge the dog was the only casualty on the Rouge River during Hurricane Hazel. We were all shuttled to safety eventually with a much more powerful boat driven by Murray Brown of Murdon Marine, Port Carling. Murray was a volunteer fireman in West Rouge at that time.

"I went to work the next morning, a Saturday, remorseful over the loss of my boat and motor. In the afternoon, I went down to the Rouge and was greatly surprised to see that the water had completely receded, leaving a devastation of caved-in houses and cottages with a layer of silt two to three inches thick over the whole valley.

"I walked down the road toward our saviour tree, which was an odd-shaped cedar, and the last time I was down that way, it was still there. A little further on, there was my boat caught in a wire fence with the motor attached, and of course full of silt. Jammed under the seat was an Eveready lamp, still faintly glowing."

Across large areas of the province the hurricane's passage caused inconvenience. In Belleville, Friday-night movie crowds stumbled their way out of theatres that went completely dark when fallen hydro lines cut off power. For some time telephone lines were out, too. Fallen trees blocked Highways 2 and 4. At Kingston, the OPP were warning all motorists off the highways. Trees five feet in diameter had been toppled by the winds. Lindsay, Janetville, Port Perry, all suffered power failures. Farms, homes, stores, railway tracks, bridges, and highways all suffered the hurricane's onslaught.

Six miles east of Kitchener, John Randall's farm at Breslau, the scene of an International Ploughing Match, was a heartbreaking shambles. The tent city was virtually demolished as a 65-mile-an-hour wind blew down 100 tents and left most of the remaining 150 a sodden, tangled mess of canvas.

In many areas, Hydro men worked round the clock. Firemen, too, were heavily in demand, particularly in Grand Valley, where about fifty homes had three or four feet of water in the ground floor. The Grand River rose ten inches in twenty minutes, and the 27-man fire brigade spent all night rescuing marooned residents.

But it was the Humber River valley, and especially the area around Woodbridge, that suffered something far worse than inconvenience, as the rest of the stories in this chapter attest.

It was just outside Woodbridge where Howard Monahan, an experienced car-transport driver inching his way cautiously home, felt something tell him to stop. He walked to the front of his truck, saw the lights of an oncoming car start onto the bridge before him, and then the bridge went out. His wife passes on the story: "The car was on its nose in the river and it was going to go any-time. He said he never felt so helpless in his life – he and the people with him could just stand and watch. Then he saw someone climb out the back window, grab hold of the roof, and get onto the trunk. It looked like a girl, but it could have been a woman; they thought they saw three people in the car before the bridge went out, but they weren't sure. Anyway, the girl climbed up the broken parts of the bridge and ran down the road. A little while later she came back with a tow truck and a couple of men with some extra rope. The girl tied the rope around her waist and got onto the car again; she helped the other passengers out, and though he wasn't sure, he thought one was carrying a child. Just as they got the last one on the bridge, the car left with another flood."

According to one resident, in Woodbridge itself the Humber, normally 65 feet wide, swelled to 350 feet at the narrowest point. It left 10 dead and 250 homeless and flooded one-third of the community of Woodbridge and Pine Grove. "Damage to commercial and industrial property in Woodbridge alone was estimated at $550,000. Sidewalks were uprooted, sewage and water mains broken. At midnight Friday, with the flood rising to a peak, the town's water supply was contaminated and power disrupted.

"More than 4,000 gallons of pure water reached the town in two Toronto street-flushing tank trucks Saturday morning. Under police and Red Cross supervision, pails of pure water were doled out to the residents."

Mary Wood recalls that a typhoid outbreak was feared, and 650 residents were inoculated in a six-hour blitz of local doctors. Rescue operations involved naval units, who rowed 27-foot whalers through flooded areas picking up stranded residents.

Lieutenant John P. Connor was in command of the Royal Canadian Sea Cadet Corps "Ark Royal" at the time, and promptly responded with two 27-foot whalers to the call to Woodbridge. "Once in Woodbridge we were placed under command of the Fire Department and were assigned street detail. Our purpose was to walk alongside of the whalers and check houses for stranded inhabitants. The water was fast-moving and chest-deep and it took a dozen people to guide the craft through the current. One learned very quickly to keep a good grasp of the boat, as unseen culverts caused more than one temporary disappearance of the crew.

"The most memorable event at this point was rescuing an 82-year-old bed-ridden grandmother – mattress and all, and her son who, two days before, had been discharged from hospital, having been confined for pneumonia. The son's activities were memorable as well. He stayed on his front porch all night, and with the aid of a broomstick, he personally rescued twenty-seven cats and fourteen dogs. All were loaded aboard the whaler and the menagerie huddled together for warmth. Not so much as a hiss, scratch, growl, or bark occurred. When we reached high ground near the Fire Hall, our cargo of cats and dogs were last seen heading for still higher ground – but still together."

On another occasion, a "very large fireman" and Lieutenant Connor clambered across a bridge made from a fire-truck ladder, just inches above a roaring current, to reach a stranded household: "The house contained newborn twins and there was no way that food and milk supplies could be delivered, so evacuation was ordered. The male occupant was happy to see us since we could help him carry his TV set upstairs so he could watch the hockey game. He was obviously a sports-minded individual since the fireman located a baseball bat near the front door. The dialogue that ensued gave little doubt as to what the fireman had in mind, or the time limit required of the occupant to make the more appropriate choice. We safely removed two very young babies, and two very vocal adults."

Every four hours the rescue groups working with the whalers were sent to the Fire Hall to dry their clothes and have hot food and drinks. Lieutenant Connor (now the marketing manager for a large printing company) still remembers how graciously the ladies serving the drinks and food ignored the fact that their customers were half naked as their clothes dried in another room.

The service clubs and women's organizations served a thousand meals a day for two weeks to the homeless and to rescue workers, while companies like Simpsons and Westinghouse helped to furnish the emergency mobile homes set up in the Agricultural Fair grounds.

The community spirit seems to have been truly admirable. After burying her mother (a widow of seventy-seven who died of natural causes on October 16), Mrs. Wood and her family, "my husband, my brothers, and their wives, went directly to my mother's home and sorted clothing, dishes, household things, etc., and took them to the public places receiving same for the flood victims."

Joan Franklin was one of the people helped by such kindness. On October 15 she was living in a mobile-home park in Woodbridge. There had been high-water warnings on radio during the day and toward evening the water in the park had risen two feet, and was up to the steps of their home. Mr. Franklin had not yet arrived home when, later in the evening, a neighbour warned Joan she would have to seek safety on higher ground. Mrs. Franklin, her year-old son Michael, and a number of others from the trailer park found refuge with kind people who had a house at the top of a hill overlooking the park.

Next morning they found most of the mobile homes (twenty, according to Mrs. Wood's records) had been swept downriver to a bend and there piled up like so many matchboxes. Fortunately, the Franklin home had lodged against a tree and had not moved very far. Although the Franklins went down to their trailer as quickly as possible, they found that looters had already taken some booty. Mrs. Franklin's entire set of "good" dishes was gone, but they did as good a job as possible of salvaging things from the waters and later tackled the job of cleaning out the fine silt that was embedded in everything. Mr. Franklin was able to repair many of the electrical appliances. The major, lasting, positive feeling about the whole Hazel episode came in connection with the trailer itself: the company took it back to the factory and completely rebuilt it for the Franklins. And the flood fund, to which so many people donated, reimbursed the young couple for their losses.

Mrs. May Lovett remembers vividly the experience that her sister had with the Woodbridge flood: "She was sitting in the livingroom and her husband was on the night shift in Malton. She looked up and saw water coming across the floor; she woke the children and put some clothes on them and then hurried out onto the veranda in the front. The street was already flooded, so they climbed on the railing.

"While they were there, some men came and got their boat which was fastened in the backyard. It was a large boat but when they came around to the street it was already loaded. They yelled at my sister to get in but she refused, as she knew it was overloaded. Just then it upset and all were drowned.

"She and the children stood on the veranda rail all

night, until firemen rescued them in the morning. She said it was a problem keeping the children awake as they were so young, but she managed by talking and telling them stories all night."

Cecil Rowe, the Woodbridge postmaster, was busy warning cars away from a bridge that was a foot under water. He thought he had succeeded in persuading a couple from the village, who were driving their seven-year-old daughter and the pet dog to safety, to take the long way round. Then "they suddenly roared off to get across the bridge. At the moment they hit the centre, a great flood-crest hit the bridge, tearing the railings down and sweeping the car and occupants away." In Mr. Rowe's sad words: "We could see the headlights bobbing for the longest time and could only guess at the terror they felt. They were found drowned the next day."

The grim aftermath. A body is hoisted to the Bloor Street bridge from the Humber River. *Photo: Toronto Star*

Crushed into a shapeless hunk of metal, the fire truck on which five men lost their lives sits in the middle of the receding river. *Photo: Toronto Star*

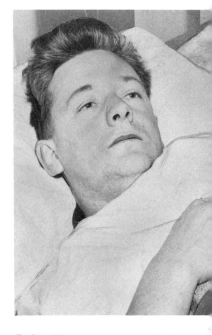

(Left) The programme of the memorial service for the firemen who lost their lives. **(Above)** Jack Phillips, one of the volunteer firemen who swam to safety when the truck was engulfed. *Photo: Toronto Star*

After the storm, volunteers tackled the receding floodwaters by boat or on foot in a cold and bitter search for bodies. *Photos: Toronto Telegram, York University Archives*

(Top) The awesome power of the floods caused by Hurricane Hazel is hard to comprehend. This picture gives some idea of the forces involved. **(Bottom)** From crushed houses like this, only a pitiful amount could be salvaged. The man in the raincoat is Joseph Ward, recovered from his harrowing night on the roof-top. *Photos: Toronto Telegram, York University Archives*

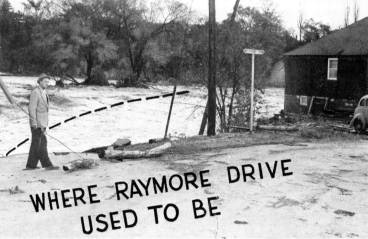

This view from downriver shows clearly what happened to Raymore Drive when the Humber River burst its banks and swept straight across the point of land where the street was built. The photograph below demonstrates how completely the houses were wiped off the map, with terrible loss of life. *Photos: Toronto Star*

(Top) The swollen Humber River thunders by. One bystander remembers that it sounded "like a freight train". *Photo courtesy of Roger E. Britnell* **(Bottom)** This is all the river left of one Raymore Drive home. Bill Birch, one of the hundreds of volunteers working in the clean-up operation, disbelievingly peers inside. *Photo: Toronto Star*

The Don River was not to be outdone. Here Jim McArthur (whose escape from the Don Valley is described in the book) indicates the height reached on his house by the floodwaters. *Photo courtesy of Jim McArthur*

Where Yonge Street crossed the Don at Hogg's Hollow, the damage was devastating. The Yonge Street bridge was washed out and had to be replaced by a Bailey bridge; the area of the Jolly Miller Tavern was totally awash, and scores of fine houses along the banks had their foundations scoured out from beneath them. *Photo courtesy of Frank W. Roberts*

The *Toronto Star* headlines tell the story—and so does the face of little Nancy Thorpe, orphaned by the storm.   *Photo: Toronto Star*

FIVE VOLUNTEER FIREMEN

For the volunteer firemen who manned all the township fire brigades in the early 1950s, Friday night was like any other. They were on call twenty-four hours a day, seven days a week. They might regularly be employed as electricians, car salesmen, or butchers, but at the sound of the siren from the fire hall there was instant response. As one fireman put it, "If a fireman was carving a roast of beef for a customer, the knife was dropped, boots jumped into, apron still tied around the middle, and away he went to the fire."

"That was just the way it was," recalls Bryan Mitchell, a volunteer fireman of the time. "It was a way of life for us. You didn't respond that often in the course of the year, perhaps thirty-five to forty times. But we left our beds on cold winter nights, out into five and ten below zero weather, drove our cars to the station, and got onto the truck for another cold drive to the fire."

During that Friday, October 15, the Royal York station, where Mitchell was assigned, began receiving numerous calls reporting flooded basements. Since fire trucks and pumps could scarcely be deployed to pump out basements, these calls were referred to the works department. At 4:30 p.m., a call came from police, reporting people trapped on the top of a car which had become stalled in water in an underpass. When Bryan Mitchell suggested they would be better served by the New Toronto brigade which had an aerial ladder, he was astonished to be told that the other brigade had already been called, and their aerial ladder was now buried in a hole in a collapsed section of the road. Mitchell then dispatched Captain McFadden, a crew, and the ladder truck and waited and waited an interminable time for word by radio of their arrival at the scene.

Traffic moved at a crawl. Roads and ditches were covered with water, making it necessary to take sightings on the hydro poles to determine that you were still on the road. When the fire truck did arrive at the scene, the car had disappeared. Incredibly, it was completely submerged in the water collected in the underpass. The passengers had climbed out onto the hood of a large furniture van and, finally, pursued by the rising water, onto the van's roof. From that height a rescue was not easy, and it was after 6:30 when, with the aid of ladders and ropes, the motorists were brought to safety. For the firemen it was merely a prelude to what the night would bring.

Several small fires, problems with the siren alarm system, the powerful wind, and wires down everywhere made it what Mitchell called "a dirty night", though "hurricane" would not have been the word that entered his thoughts. It was 11:15, on a night already filled with a series of emergencies, when the police hot line requested the brigade ladder truck up at Raymore Drive.

Like Bryan Mitchell, James Dalgleish Britton was a volunteer fireman, having joined the fire department when he was sixteen. The war was on at the time, and the department needed volunteers. James "took the opportunity" because he was too young to go to war. When the first, newly formed, paid department began in June 1953, he became a Captain. It tells a good deal about James Britton that he continued to serve as a volunteer with the Lambton Mills group.

While Mitchell was responding to the Raymore Drive call, fireman Britton, Deputy Chief Clarence "Tiny" Collins, and firemen Angus Small, Roy Oliver, Dave and Marsh Palmateer, Jack Phillips, and Frank Mercer answered a call about two people trapped in a car by the Humber River, on the section between Dundas south to Old Mill Road.

On this stretch of the Humber, the normally tranquil little river flows through a flat valley that has precipitous, almost cliff-like banks on either side. Down in the valley a roadway runs parallel to the river about a hundred yards west of it, with the very steep, hundred-foot riverbank about the same distance further west. Atop that embankment, and set well back from its edge, are fine homes on a winding residential street. One of the largest homes is the Boylens', a familiar landmark in the neighbourhood.

For fireman James Britton, this was familiar territory. He knew the valley well. He grew up here. Fireman Britton was driving the truck that night, and as he drove down into the valley, the water had risen so high it was fuming white all across the road. They were only about a quarter of the way into the valley, just back of the Boylen place, but could see there was no way they could go on driving into the rapidly rising water.

Britton says they could see the car they were supposed to rescue, but there was no one in it. The people were gone. "Next thing we know, we're in trouble."

Frank Mercer, who had been a volunteer fireman in years past, just happened to be on the scene that night, instead of being at his house and store in Huntsville. In his own car he had followed his friends on the fire truck down the river road, to lend assistance if he could. Now he found the rapidly rising floodwaters pushing his car into the back of the fire truck, and in a matter of minutes his car was being swept sideways off the road. Only by catching a rope thrown by the firemen was Mercer able to extricate himself from the car and make it to the fire truck. As his friends helped him clamber aboard, they watched his car in disbelief. As Britton remembers, "His car went sideways against a bunch of trees. It was like Niagara Falls hitting the car broadside. Behind us you couldn't see the road any more."

He pauses, reliving the whole scene in his mind. "Well, what are we going to do? There's nothing behind us. You can't see the road any more. The water is all around you."

The memory is a vivid one and a painful one. His voice chokes with emotion, and he has trouble getting the words out. He apologizes and goes on.

"What are you going to do? We parked the truck. The water is getting higher and higher. You know, I grew up here. Oh, we've seen the Humber in flood. We used to go down, little bare-assed kids . . . to play off the islands. As we figured, O.K., fine. But the water kept coming. Up to the tires. Getting higher. And higher. But you know, Tiny and all those guys, we *know* this river. We were getting concerned. But we weren't upset."

The men decided they had better call the police and let them know where they were. In those days the firemen put their calls through the police department radio, so there was no problem in getting the call through. Then, having made sure all the truck lights, front, back, and spotlights, were full on to show rescuers exactly where they were, the men sat on top of the truck and waited.

A short time later dark figures could be seen making their way down the steep embankment, thrusting a small rowboat ahead of them – policemen and firemen coming promptly to the aid of their friends. The relief of the men aboard the truck was short-lived. As soon as the rescue boat hit the water, it was sent spinning crazily on the current and was swamped.

At the bottom of the Boylen property was a chain-link fence, and Britton decided to try to reach that fence. While no rope aboard the truck could span the distance to the fence, he decided to use what rope there was as a safety measure, and tied one end around his waist. With a pike pole in hand to provide some leverage against the current, he stepped cautiously off the fire truck. He managed no more than a step or two when the current swept his feet out from under him, and, arms flailing, he was hauled back aboard the fire truck. No chance of escape that way.

Fireman Dave Palmateer retrieved the rope, tied it to the end of a hose, and began coiling the rope.

Britton recalls simply: "When we realize . . . well obviously the water's coming up, eh? It ain't going down . . . it's just plain coming up. There wasn't much conversation. Just a sorting out of who could swim and who couldn't, and a divvying up of anything that would float. Marsh could swim; Jack Phillips could swim; Angus couldn't swim. . . . "

With only the eerie lights of the fire truck poking beams into the pitch black of the night, the firemen sat in a circle on top of the truck, watching the water climb towards them, minute by minute.

Britton continues, "Then what happened was that the water took our hose out! It just went out like a snake, all joined in one piece. Gone! You wouldn't believe it. We're starting to float! We shook hands . . . then every man for himself."

Three major currents had developed in the flood-swollen river: two rushing out towards midstream, one that went in closer to the high bank. When Britton jumped off the truck, he was aiming for the high-bank side of the river.

Firemen Britton, Marsh Palmateer, and Phillips were the lucky ones, caught up in the current that took them closest to shore. Britton's maroon-coloured jacket, with leather sleeves and tight leather wristbands, acted like a lifejacket, all puffed up with air.

Britton continues, "I was on my back, going downstream head first. And all of a sudden something hit me in the face. I grabbed for it and I spun right around, and I found myself under a big tree. I don't know how far I'd be from shore, but between me and the shore was like . . . well, I keep saying Niagara Falls. You wouldn't believe it! No way I can jump it. No way I'm going to let go. . . . I'm on this beautiful big tree. . . . I'm sitting up there, and I'm hanging on, you damn well better believe it.

"I'm above the water at this point. And all of a sudden I hear this moaning. And here's this guy . . . he's hanging onto a little sapling. His head's just above water."

Britton thought at first it was Tiny Collins, but then discovered it was Frank Mercer, the former volunteer fireman who had just happened to come along behind the fire truck on its call to the river, eager to help. He was two or three arm's lengths away, but Britton thought he could catch hold of Frank's foot. There were policemen on shore with flashlights, so Britton felt there was a good chance of help arriving soon.

"Frank, for God's sake, give me your foot. Get your foot up here and I'll grab it," he urged. "And he just got a funny look on his face and went down the tree like this, and ahh . . . he's gone.

"The policemen threw me a rope. And I don't remember hitting shore, because they just gave one yank and I didn't go through the water . . . I went straight through the air. Boom! That was it. I came home, had a warm bath, and went back to work."

Firemen Small, Collins, Palmateer, Mercer, and Roy Oliver would never go home again. When Dave Palmateer's body was found several days later, he had rope burns, and the rope he had been coiling, just as the hoses were swept from the fire engine, was wrapped tightly around him.

The fire engine which had bobbed grotesquely downstream, its lights miraculously still blazing during the early part of its voyage, was found just beyond the stone bridge, nearly half a mile downstream at the Old Mill parking lot. The ladders had been ripped off, the engine hood crushed in. But the tires were intact, and the radio, which was cut out with a torch, still worked.

As for the call that took five firemen on their last rescue mission, this remained something of a mystery. The people who were reported stranded by the Humber never did come forward, if they themselves survived. Roxena Pearl Collins, widow of Tiny Collins, says today that four young people came to the funeral parlour and just "hung around for a while". No one knew who they were. They talked with her, but never identified themselves. She didn't have the presence of mind to ask at the time, but has often wondered since if they might have been the people from the car.

"Roxy" Collins still has terribly vivid recollections of that night. She and her husband had been out earlier in the evening and had just come home shortly after 1:00 a.m., and gone to bed, when the siren went. When she wakened about 4:00 a.m. and saw lights still on, her first thought was, "Those guys . . . they're sitting down at the firehall talking, I'll bet."

Before she could phone the firehall, her sister-in-law phoned to say that Tiny was "marooned" in the Humber. Over the next anxious hours, there were phone calls and visits from clergymen; as late as 4:00 the next afternoon, Red Cross and radio reports were still suggesting some of these men were "at outposts".

Even today it's an emotional thing for Mrs. Collins to remember how she finally got on the phone to the radio station and burst out, "Will you stop telling me that. You know there's no outpost. What are you talking about? They're *drowned*!"

For Lillian Small memories of that day and night are still deeply etched. Angus, her husband, had been working out of town. He was building a house for Lillian's sister, so he had come down from Orangeville early in the evening. Lillian was concerned about the weather and anxious for his safety. She remembers the sound of the storm as eerie: "The weirdest sound. I'll never forget it. It seemed to be in the air. Not like a siren, but a sort of whistling sound. It just made you shiver. And the sky looked so funny."

Late in the evening, Angus Small got a call for help from his son who was with a friend whose car had gotten stuck in the mud. While returning with his son, fireman Small responded to the siren call for volunteers, so he did not return to his home. His son drove the family car home. When someone came to her door to tell her of the accident, Lillian Small could not get it through her mind that their car was there in the driveway, but her husband was not home.

Lillian Small has never remarried and now lives alone in the same house in Etobicoke where she and her family lived during Hazel. Twenty-five years after the hurricane that took her husband's life, she says, "Every time there's a heavy wind whistling, it always kind of reminds me of it. I don't care for the wind ever since then. . . . "

The wives shared in the remarkable esprit de corps of the firemen, and Mrs. Collins to this day praises the other women for their concern and consideration. The widows of those five firemen who lost their lives in the Humber were given $25 a month by the Borough. It has become $32.50 today.

Fireman Bryan Mitchell, son of a fire chief, is today himself Fire Chief of the Etobicoke Fire Department. Whatever the pull of the occupation that calls men to danger and to risk their lives, it often seems to run in families.

"Going back even to those volunteer days. We used to get 75 cents for a house fire. So here you are, Sunday, you've got your nice new suit on, and the siren goes. You run over to the fire hall. It costs you 75 cents to get the suit cleaned," recalls fireman Britton.

James Dalgleish Britton still lives in Etobicoke today, still fights fires, still has an unusual sense of community spirit. He's much involved with Big Brothers and the Cubs. If you ask Britton today what makes a man become a fireman, he pauses and says, "That's a damn hard question to answer. I got involved in it because I had an obligation, and because I was there, and because I could do it."

Britton is direct and straightforward in his recollection of the loss of his friends. "I was proud of them," he says. "It's like a soldier; he was called on to do a job and he did it, and he did it well. That's the answer. That's the only way to put it."

CHAPTER EIGHT

AN ORPHAN OF THE STORM

The Clifford Thorpes lived on Island Road with their two children, Bobby, aged two, and Nancy, just four months old. On the night of Hazel, the children's grandmother was visiting the family. As the waters of Etobicoke Creek began to rise, the young couple called the Long Branch volunteer fire department for help. Fire Chief Albert Houston and a number of men, including volunteers Cecil Lane and Norm Clift, set out for Island Road, south of Lakeshore Road and one street west of the Creek, to rescue, as fireman Lane recalls, "a baby". They were to pick up the baby and bring her back to Lakeshore Road, where they were to meet someone who would take the child into the city.

You are left to wonder why this special effort on the part of parents who must have sensed danger was directed just to their infant daughter and not to their young son and themselves. Perhaps they felt that as adults, they were not in any real danger. And perhaps they did plan to send little Bobby along with baby Nancy, and the child protested tearfully that he didn't want to leave.

By the time the Long Branch fire truck reached Island Road, the street was already under so much water, the firemen abandoned their truck in favour of a city dump truck which they commandeered. Here Norm Clift takes up the story: "If I remember right there were ten or twelve of us – three in the cab and the balance in the box. We then started down the road and our first stop was at a cottage-style home whose older residents [the Thorpes] refused to be evacuated on the grounds of having gone through floods before and going to ride this one out also. But as they had a young baby they asked us to see that it (I think it was a girl) could be cared for, and had a small valise with bottles full of formula packed. Two of the firemen waded through chest-high water to get the baby and the case, and brought them back to the truck." In fact, we know that Fire Chief Houston was one of the men, and that they clung to a rope tied between the truck and the Thorpe house, to avoid being swept away by the current.

"The water kept rising and to the point of stalling the motor; we finally cut the fan belt off. That worked for a short while and we managed to drive further down the road where we rescued two people from marooned cars. Then the motor stalled and the current bumped us still further down the road and we finally came to rest next to a big oak tree. There was also a house some twenty-five feet from us and a car on its front lawn. Next door was a cement-block house with an exceptionally high basement and a good sound roof. But as we were marooned on this truck with some five and a half to six feet of water all around us we were literally at the mercy of the river. Finally somebody with a cedar-strip boat came by and took some four firemen and the two rescued persons from the car and the young Thorpe baby to the roof of the cement-block house."

The boat tried to return to the truck for the stranded firemen but the current smashed it to pieces against the truck and the boatmen were glad to scramble aboard with the firemen. Norm Clift continues: "There we conversed in shouting voices, telling them how much of the parked car was still visible. It seems we first noticed the door handles disappear, then it was halfway up the windows, then to the roof, and I imagine it was around 3:00 or 4:00 a.m. there was only a spot of the roof showing. Then the spot began to get bigger and bigger and we knew the crest had been reached.

"During our stay in the truck and as the depth of the water got worse, we could see big mobile trailers from the trailer grounds north of the bridge on Lakeshore Road bouncing down the river and hear dishes, cups, pots, and pans bouncing off shelves. We could also hear people screaming for help, but we were helpless to do a thing. At one point, there were flashes up the river as hydro lines snapped and fell into the water.

"The damage and sight of what that hurricane did was ghastly. Homes were knocked off their foundations, cars were flooded and filled with silt, roots and debris was all around. And the home of the people – all three or four – where we rescued the baby was completely gone – only the solid concrete steps remained."

When morning came, the Thorpe house was gone. Etobicoke Creek had swept it away. Of the whole Thorpe family, only four-month-old Nancy survived.

In the morning light, when the floods had receded to a depth of four feet or so, a front-end loader made its way down the street. The people from the rooftops stepped into its scoop and were then brought to safety. In the same unconventional manner, the firemen were taken from the top of the truck.

Sixteen-year-old Sylvia Jones was one of the people rescued in this way. Early in the flood her father had put a ladder up to their roof and it had been gratefully used by neighbours. Eventually, thirty-two soaked and shivering people and three dogs spent the long, wet night perched on that rooftop. Among them was little Nancy Thorpe.

Sylvia Jones, now Mrs. Cutajar, remembers vividly how that came about: "Just across the street from us three houses were washed out into the lake taking the lives of Pat and Cliff Thorpe, their son Bobby, also Pat's mother, Mrs. Johnson. I was given the baby, Nancy, by a fireman, who had tried to rescue the family when the water trapped them in their home. The baby's mother had wrapped her warmly and I held her in my arms all night. She was a tiny little girl; she was a premature baby and was fed at frequent times. Nancy slept most of the night with no feedings till she reached the hospital the next morning. While the water was all around our house, trailer homes were sailing past the house, hitting hydro poles and breaking them off, and the wires were hitting the water with a spray of sparks.

"We were rescued in the morning by a group of people and driven to the highway, where I handed Nancy over to a Red Cross worker. I identified the baby as Nancy Thorpe and told them that her parents had been lost in the flood. She was then taken to St. Joseph's Hospital for an examination, and was found to be in good health."

Some days later the Thorpe family dog reappeared. When he was taken to where baby Nancy lay, he crawled under the covers with the child.

What happened to the orphan of Hurricane Hazel, now a young woman of twenty-five, has deliberately been kept private. One person who does know her story feels that silence on the subject is his obligation, and his preference.

CHAPTER NINE

THE HOLLAND MARSH

Twenty-five miles north of Toronto lies some of the richest farmland in the country. Bordering the Holland River, which meanders its lazy way into Lake Simcoe, the 10,000-acre flatland is known as the "Holland Marsh". River and marshlands were named, not, as popularly believed, to commemorate the pioneer Dutch settlers, but to honour Major J. S. Holland, who made the Upper Canada survey of the wilds of York in the late 1700s. The first settlers must have been people of imagination and vision to see possibilities in thirty square miles of marsh grass, home to muskrats, frogs, and giant mosquitoes. With pioneer ingenuity those Canadians of long ago built two sawmills in the area, trapped the muskrats, and harvested the marsh hay with mowers pulled by horses with snowshoe-like boards on their feet. The large wooden shoes kept the horses from sinking in the bog and the animals became so accustomed to that security, oldtimers say, they wouldn't go near the marsh without them. In the late 1800s and the early years of this century, the crop of marsh hay was cut, cured, dried, and used for mattress stuffing. But as agricultural land the marsh was considered useless.

96

A Bradford grocer, D. W. (Dave) Watson, had a dream about being able to drain the marsh. He interested Professor W. H. Day of the Guelph Agricultural College in the project, back in 1910, when the land was worth about a dollar an acre. It was thought that if the land could be reclaimed, the value would be increased, possibly to as much as $40 or $50 an acre, and that a variety of crops could be taken off. As it did with so many dreams, the First World War put an end to any practical efforts on that project. But Professor Day was persistent, and more than a decade after the original small beginnings, some two hundred acres were drained near Bradford and the first crops were harvested in 1927.

In 1929 contractors Cummings and Robinson went ahead with a full drainage scheme. The value of the contract was $237,000, or $21 per acre of land actually reclaimed. The Ontario government paid twenty per cent and the local municipalities took up the rest. J. F. Hambly, Reeve of West Gwillimbury, L. A. Neilly (Gilford), Percy Selby, W. J. Gales, and Herman Lennox, Councillors, were all associated with the drainage scheme.

It wasn't until 1934 that the first handful of year-round settlers, eighteen Dutch families including a young man named John Van Dyke, moved into the area so laboriously reclaimed from swamp water. With a government gift of lumber the settlers erected their first school, S.S. No. 16, with all voluntary labour – with the exception of Anthony Sweep, who assumed the role of chief carpenter and overseer for the magnificent sum of 75 cents an hour.

Over the years the community grew with an influx of families from many parts of Europe, until in that October of 1954, some 3,000 people lived in the Holland Marsh area. They were industrious farm people, whose produce of fresh fruits and vegetables was shipped to markets many hundreds of miles away. Because of the wet weather that year the farmers were about two weeks behind with their harvest. But in another week some 500,000 bags of onions, almost as many crates of celery, and millions of bushels of other vegetables would be ready for shipping – the final autumn harvest.

Let John Van Dyke take up the story in his own words: "Then came October 15, the day that it did not rain, but poured, all day long. There was no let-up and by late afternoon the soil was completely saturated. The drainage river within the boundary of the Marsh was overflowing, as were the drainage ditches, and water spilled over on some of the low-lying fields. The highlands surrounding the Marsh could not absorb all this rain, and since the land slopes down towards the Marsh the drainage canal was filling up fast, the water pressing against the dikes.

"By early evening came the danger point. Water had reached the top and in some places came over the top and all able-bodied men were summoned to come out to sandbag the weak spots. But the water rose so rapidly, these efforts were soon abandoned and the people were told to get out and go to higher ground.

"So most of the residents did just that and made their way to the town of Bradford which is located high on a hill an average of five miles distant. People just poured into the little town – a real invasion. If ever there was a showing of real community spirit, an effort to help a neighbour in need, in the history of the town of Bradford, then it was on the night of October 15, 1954."

No family in the Holland Marsh area that night went through an experience as traumatic as Harry de Peuter's family. Ironically, the de Peuters had arrived in Canada in May 1954 after surviving the terrible 1953 floods in Holland which drowned 2,500 people. The de Peuters –

father, mother, and twelve children ranging in age from nineteen to eighteen months – soon established themselves on the Marsh at Springdale, west of Highway 400, where they lived in a two-storey house and worked on a farm.

Early in the evening of Hurricane Hazel the farm's foreman dropped in to warn them that the Marsh might flood, but that if so, they would be looked after. Like the rest of the family, 15-year-old Harry was not overly worried. "After all, we were 1,500 miles away from the ocean, and the ocean was where the floods came from."

Close to 9 o'clock, however, Harry, his elder brother, and a visiting friend were sent off to the local store to get candles in case the storm caused a power failure. When they reached the store they were astonished to find the doors wide open, and everyone gone. They helped themselves to candles (planning to pay later) and set out back home.

At this point things became serious. The water was now running over the road, and the wind was so strong that the boys had to hold hands as they walked. They noticed that the only lights around came from their house, and realized that everyone else had cleared out.

Back in the house they held a family conference and decided that with only five adults and twelve children they were not in a position to make a break for higher ground. Now the water was flowing into the house, and floating onion crates began to bang into the back door, forcing it open. Harry's father finally decided to nail the door shut with a board, which was "our first big mistake, since it meant that the water level rose higher outside the house than inside."

There was two feet of water in the house and the furniture had been stacked on tables when from upstairs the family saw a neighbouring house start to move. Then as they felt "a terrific jolt" they realized that *they* were moving, floating off the pilings that formed the house's base. "The amazing part was," Harry recalls, "all the lights in the house stayed on, because we were moving towards the hydro lines, and they were slackening."

Then the house hit the road and a hydro pole, shearing it right off and dropping the wires on to the roof, where they lay shooting sparks all over the place. For a while it seemed that the weight of the wires over one corner might tip the house over, but then, with another jolt, the house was free.

"The house just took off like a boat, a real Noah's Ark. From 11:30 till 6:30 we floated aimlessly through the Marsh, bumping into houses, greenhouses, barns, hydro poles, everything. The area over by the Holland River had a faster current and somehow our house got caught in that current and started spinning like a top, faster and faster, and rocking to and fro. We all – all fifteen of us – would run from one side of the house to the other when it tilted, trying to balance it out. One of my younger brothers, Bastian, actually got violently sea-sick.

"Until then we had been too busy to really worry and then one of the younger ones asked if we were all going to die. My mother said that only one person knew that, the Lord, and we all knelt down and prayed, the Lord's Prayer. And we did get out of the current and finally came to rest against a service road near the 400, where a complete field of carrots had floated up to the surface and helped hold us in place. We were two and a half miles away from where we started, with lots of side trips that had often taken us near our original place.

"At that time there were still cars going along the 400 and we shouted and waved to attract their attention. I even fired off a .22, but with the noise of the wind and the water, it couldn't be heard. Then we waved bedsheets and motorists saw us, and soon an amphibious truck from Camp Borden came along. One man got out, tied a rope around his waist, and plunged in to swim towards our house. We were about 250 feet away and the water was pretty wild and cold but he made it. We knocked a window out downstairs and pulled him in. Then another man came along the rope in a canoe which kept tipping but he told us we'd be okay with the extra weight of two people in the canoe. So we made it out to the truck in seven trips, and were taken to Bradford, where we stayed in the Bradford Town Hall.

"We never found out the name of the man who swam out with the rope to rescue us. Then one day my brother was in Barrie, in Jack Oates' paint store, and he got talking about the wet weather and how it wasn't as bad as Hurricane Hazel and one thing led to another and they found out that he, Jack Oates, was the man who had saved us."

Allan Anderson, then a CBC broadcaster, was one of the first outsiders to reach Bradford the next day. "It was unbelievable," he recalls. "The Marsh was just one vast lake. All you could see in the distance sticking out of the water was the steeple of the Springdale Christian Reform Church. In Bradford itself it was like a war zone. The flood victims had been taken into people's homes and the town was bursting at the seams. The town hall was full of people sleeping, crowded so close together you thought that they were almost sleeping standing up."

Food and clothing were also provided for the flood victims by the good ladies of the town, which opened its heart to its flooded neighbours, as did the town of Schomberg. Robert Evans, then a high-school student, was astonished to wake up in his Bradford home the morning after the hurricane and find another family sleeping there. The evacuees, who spoke Dutch but very little English, stayed with his family for about a week.

John Van Dyke is still deeply grateful for the many kindnesses shown to the refugees. He recalls the feeling of the morning of October 16. "The day before, the Marsh still held the promise of a good supply of vegetables for the food markets of Canada and abroad – now it had once more turned into a lake. Practically the entire crop found a watery grave; very little could be salvaged.

"Many homes too were either ruined or badly damaged and the furniture beyond repair. This was especially true on the Springdale side, west of Highway 400, where the water rose as high as fifteen feet, flowing clean over the highway. Two or three homes were lifted off their foundations and set afloat. They travelled for about a mile, coming to rest against a highway. One of these homes even contained an entire family" – as Harry de Peuter knew only too well.

In all, five hundred homes were destroyed, although miraculously no lives were lost. These were people who well understood the threat of water; as the floodtide rose, farm families waded to safety or were rescued from their homes by neighbours and boats. George Bryant, covering the event for the *Toronto Daily Star*, wrote that opportunities for heroism are rare, but on that night there were so many opportunities and so many heroes that heroism became commonplace.

John Van Dyke was able to note a biological mystery. "Here and there an outhouse, of which there were a good many in those days, had been picked up by the flood-waters and carried gently to a new location, where it could not be of service to the original owners any more. How they got along without this precious little building one can only guess!" In fact, an unexpected side effect of Hurricane Hazel was the introduction of inside plumbing to many areas of the Marsh that had hitherto gone without. More immediate needs were met by the importation of a hundred portable toilets. Kathleen Short of the Red Cross made this vital delivery by truck from the Long Branch Army Depot. When the trip took all night, her mother angrily commented: "One of these days all these late nights will catch up with you!"

More seriously, John Van Dyke notes that "all vegetables or any food that had been in contact with the flood water had to be destroyed. Hundreds and hundreds of tons of vegetables were taken to be dumped. All roads leading out of the Marsh were closely guarded twenty-four hours a day, and nobody was allowed to transport produce from the area without authorization. The men on guard duty were mostly Marsh farmers sworn in as temporary police, and they took their job quite seriously. They would stop everybody – their next-door neighbours, yes, even their next of kin."

The green and fertile Holland Marsh was now a wasteland of water. Worse, it was a sea of wrecked homes, debris of all sorts, and floating, rotting vegetables. It was the smell of rotting onions that Norm Synnott remembers. He and two other teachers from Barrie were passing the marsh on Highway 400 shortly after the hurricane. "Instead of the usual expanse of black soil, we saw a great lake of water stretching to the east and to the west with the highway appearing like a causeway. Frame buildings, like derelict ships, were floating about, and the stench of rotting onions filled the air. Hundreds of sacks of onions were washed up along the embankment."

Norm Synnott disobeyed the "No Stopping" signs to snap a photograph and for his pains got a tongue-lashing from a jeep-load of soldiers "who were not fooling". He had to run for more than a mile to catch up with his car.

Jim DiCecco was a helicopter engineer who worked for the Department of Lands and Forests. He was stationed in Bancroft when, on October 16, his helicopter was ordered to the Holland Marsh. "It was a cold, grey, windy day with some showers. . . . After about six hours of flying we arrived over the Holland Marsh. Where there once was beautiful farm land, the area was now covered in water. It appeared as if Lake Simcoe had gotten bigger."

All that day Jim DiCecco's helicopter hovered over every farmhouse to make sure the house was empty, while the army, in amphibious vehicles, did the same on the water. Happily, no tragedies were discovered, despite rumours of floating bodies.

By Sunday, officials of the communities and townships, including John Smith, MP for North York, and Earl Rowe, MP for Dufferin–Simcoe, had begun the monumental task of organizing the clean-up job. Committees were struck and big George Horlings, a veteran of the Marsh and President of the Holland River Gardens Cooperative and the Marsh Commission, was appointed to head the joint committee.

The work ahead must have seemed enormous: shelter to be found for all those families; the whole bleak lake of water to be cleared, somehow, some way, and before frost came. And the big question in the minds of everyone as to whether the clearing could be done so that next spring's crops could be planted. Catastrophe enough to have lost this fall's harvest and much of the topsoil; but could that land once more be reclaimed from water to allow it to be productive again next spring?

The Holland Marsh disaster rang a bell of sympathy with the citizens of the Netherlands. From Holland, which still remembered its liberation by the Canadians in 1945 and which had been the recipient of aid from Canadians in 1952 when the lowland country was inundated, came an immediate and generous offer of help in the form of a campaign for funds in that country. Funds from government and private citizens in Canada came pouring in to help the farmers get back on their feet.

But obviously, the first priority had to be that of reclaiming their land from the waters. Robert Saunders, General Manager of Construction for Ontario Hydro, promptly offered help in draining the Marsh. Yet when the pumps were set up at the eastern end of the Marsh, they ran into trouble. The Hydro pumps were used for draining *water*: draining a marsh, awash with not only floodwaters, but tomatoes, cabbages, potatoes, onions, and carrots, to say nothing of all manner of other debris, was a different proposition.

Howard T. Harrison, with Hydro's Sir Adam Beck plant in Niagara Falls, received a call from Saunders outlining the problem, admitting they were not making any headway, and asking him to come and have a look. Harrison went to where they had sixteen pumps operating, cut all the foot-valves off, put a vacuum system in, and started all the pumps up. It worked like a charm, "and on the 13th of November I had the Holland Marsh dry."

He is generous in his praise of many who helped with the operation. Atikokan Mines and the cities of Ottawa and Montreal sent expensive equipment, paid for its transportation, and tendered no bills to anyone. It was, he says, "actually a donation from several companies and a lot of people who got together and said, 'We're going to pump out the Holland Marsh.' It was quite a project."

John Deere, Massey-Ferguson, Ford – all the industrial tractor and equipment companies – set up shop right in Bradford. All the farmers were invited to bring their equipment in there to have it rebuilt, at no charge. Meanwhile the restoration of the houses and the clearing of the land went on again.

Let John Van Dyke have the last word: "There was

real fear that for the coming two or three years very little would grow on the muck gardens. But these fears proved to be unfounded, for the very next season there was an abundant crop. The people were back to their normal way of life."

CHAPTER TEN

THE STREET THAT DISAPPEARED

Raymore Drive was a quiet little residential street, nestled against the Humber River, south of Lawrence Avenue and east of Scarlett Road. The street followed the semi-circular curve of the river and the residents prided themselves on the pleasure of the country-like living they enjoyed there. The river was familiar and loved territory to the people of Raymore Drive. Some of them had lived along its banks for fifty years. Springtime flooding was almost an annual occurrence, and in a curious way, one of those mildly hazardous shared experiences that tend to bind people together.

Perhaps this makes it somewhat more comprehensible that the Raymore Drive men and women showed little concern as the storm mounted on Friday night. Though the rains were terribly heavy, and it had been raining for what seemed days on end, this wasn't springtime, it was fall, when the river had never posed any kind of threat.

Jack Foot, who lived on Gilhaven, a street which ran into Raymore Drive, remembers there were men who came along Gilhaven and Raymore that evening, suggesting that residents seek higher ground, or go up to the Army-Navy Club on Kingdom Street. While some did take this advice, most were reassured by one long-time resident of the street, who said there had never been any real danger before. In the darkness and pelting rain, the comfort of familiar home territory was more appealing than a local hall.

It was the kind of wild, stormy night when radio or television in your own livingroom seemed a good choice. And it was the choice most people made. When the power failed around 10:30 in the evening, many turned in for the night, perhaps a little uneasy about the storm, but certainly not alarmed.

David Phillips was an eyewitness to the event that turned the river loose on Raymore Drive, the collapse of the nearby swing bridge. Coming home late from a date with his fiancée, he found his usual homeward path across the floodplain and over the swing bridge already impassable. There were police and other people gathered at the bridge; some houses were floating down the river, and some had smashed into the bridge, putting it under severe strain. Phillips crossed to the west side of the Humber, further north at Lawrence Avenue, and made his way towards his home on a hill overlooking the river and the swing bridge.

In amazement he saw the westerly abutment of the bridge tear loose, while the easterly abutment stayed firm. The wire ropes which supported the platform of the bridge itself also held, allowing the current to swing the bridge in a slight arc before it stopped in such a way that all the debris coming down the river built up against the wire ropes still connecting the westerly and easterly abutments. The normal flow of water was stopped – and the river was diverted in a tidal wave right across the floodplain that was Raymore Drive.

"The homes were literally lifted off their foundations and swept away," recalls Phillips. "You could hear the people screaming. Many of them were standing on their roofs. In many cases the screaming just stopped; the homes just disintegrated, and that was the end of it."

Fireman Bryan Mitchell, who was called to the Raymore scene, thinks many of the residents did realize the water was rising, but made poor decisions. Some of the homes rested on cement pillars, while others had full concrete basements.

"I think some of them realized their houses were moving, but a neighbour's house was on a solid foundation: therefore, they thought, 'Let's swim to the safety of the neighbour's.' That's what a lot of them did. Matter of fact as the water still rose they were right up on the rooftops of neighbours' houses, hanging onto TV aerials. Some stayed in their houses, and we could hear the screams when the houses were swept down the river with the people in them."

Mitchell remembers his fellow firemen working up to their chins in the bitterly cold water, minus their heavy boots and coats, which only hampered their efforts. He describes their efforts of trying to get life ropes to people stranded on remaining houses. The scene is vivid for him even today. "All hell broke loose," he says. "People were screaming, 'Save us. . . . Save us.' We could get spotlights on them. We could see them . . . but they were just so far out you couldn't throw ropes. We tried floating ropes to them on logs, anything buoyant. We'd grab a a piece of firewood, tie rope to it, and float it from upstream, hoping the current would get it over to them and they could tie it in some way to their house. We'd hang onto the rope on shore. Sometimes the only possibility was to swim out with a rope. We saw feats of strength we've tried to reproduce since, and we can't.

"Norm Elwin, who is now one of our district chiefs, single-handedly put up a 35-foot ladder and extended it out

horizontally to span across to a house. We've tried that
under ideal conditions at the back of the station and it's
all we can do to lift it off the ground. It's a four- or six-
man ladder. But these things happened. Everybody was
working so hard. And you could hear people screaming
. . . screaming.

"The firefighters did a good job. But for every one we
got out, there was another we couldn't get out," Mitchell
recalls sadly.

Thomas Gould and his wife Irene were among the
survivors of Raymore Drive. They had been watching
television and when the power went off, decided not to go
to bed. They heard someone shouting a warning and
opened their front door to find ankle-deep water outside.
With the water rising to their knees, and quickly to their
waists, they fled their home, rousing as many neighbours
as they could on the way.

Someone roused the Sidney Jamiesons when there
was water flowing over their front lawn. By the time they
had hastily thrown on clothes, the water was up their
four front steps and they had to be carried to safety on
the backs of rescuers.

Ed Henderson, Chester Swales, and Reginald Whibley were mentioned as tireless rescue workers, and seventeen-year-old Georgie Bridger, who waded through
waist-deep water to warn residents, was credited by Mrs.
Thomas Wakeling with saving her life. As we know from
their work with Frank Cornelius, mentioned earlier, they
certainly did save lives that terrible night.

Annie and Joe Ward lived on Raymore Drive; they
had saved for fifteen years to build their $10,000 blue and
white stucco house, and the well-tended lawn and beautiful garden were obvious evidence of how much they
cared for it. Friday afternoon, when Joe Ward came
home from DeHavilland Aircraft, he was soaked to the

skin by the heavy rains. After dinner the couple, both sixty-three years of age, settled in to watch some television. When Mrs. Ward decided to go to bed, she put Lassie, the wire-haired terrier, on her blanket at the top of the basement stairs and closed the door. Joe Ward, his feet propped on a hassock, and the blue budgie perched on his shoulder, stayed behind and finally dozed off to sleep.

When he wakened it was close to midnight. It took a moment or two to realize the TV was off, so of course that meant the hydro was off – not too alarming in view of the storm. He could hear the rain still lashing the trees and the sound of the winds, which, if anything, seemed worse than earlier in the evening. When he took his feet off the hassock and put them on the floor he was shocked to find he was standing in water, and that the water was *moving*. It was also rising. He scrambled for a flashlight, made his way quickly to the bedroom, and wakened Annie, telling her there was water in the house, she must dress quickly.

One can only imagine the thoughts that would go racing through their minds. Could they get out to safety? Would they be safer at home, upstairs, or even on the roof? Was there any safety if the water was running through their house? What must it be like outside in that blackness full of howling winds and driving rains? Joe suddenly remembered Lassie, still in the basement. He hurriedly opened the door and the wire-haired terrier swam happily out. She loved the water.

Joe, Annie, and their son had built the house on Raymore Drive, so they knew every inch of it. Joe decided the safest place would be the attic, and Annie sensibly said that if they were going to wind up marooned on a rooftop, they'd better have some food with them. The handiest thing proved to be a cherry cake from the breadbox in the kitchen. Clutching the dog and the cherry cake, and armed with a screwdriver and flash-light, the couple hastily climbed a ladder to the attic. As they climbed, they heard a tremendous crash; the huge tree that guarded the driveway had toppled before the onslaught of the winds and water, and crashed right through a windowed section of the house.

The very moment that Joe and Annie scrambled through the attic opening into the rafters of the house, the chimney crumbled and the whole house seemed to list. Time was running out, and in the cramped attic space it was easy to sense the danger of their position if the house collapsed. Using the screwdriver and his bare hands, Joe began digging frantically at the rooftop, and succeeded in making a hole large enough to squeeze through. After Annie was safely on the rooftop, Joe tried to push the dog through the small opening. It just couldn't be done, so he tenderly wrapped the dog in a blanket that was in the attic, put her on the driest part of the rafters he could find, and made his way out.

No sooner was he on the rooftop than the house gave a sort of shudder and the roof began to sink. In the wild blackness of the night it was hard to see anything. The pathetic beam of light from the flashlight didn't help very much, but it was enough to show them that their roof had hit another. They were *floating* and had rammed against another house.

The only safety now was the other roof. Holding hands and bracing themselves, the couple jumped from their sinking house to the rooftop of Molly and Jack Anderson's home. Their quickness and decisiveness saved their lives, but it was to be a long, cold night for the Wards. Annie had on just a light silk dress – the first thing that had come to hand. Joe was in lightweight slacks, shirt, and slippers – not great protection against the cold October hurricane weather.

Holding hands and clutching a breather pipe on the Andersons' roof to keep from slipping off, they watched and waited in fear and sadness. The wild, churning waters rushed a steady stream of debris and recognizable pieces of houses past them. In some of the houses that still stood they could catch a glimpse of flashlight beams moving up towards the top floors as the occupants tried to outrace the floodwaters. Most didn't make it, and from their precarious perch the Wards were witness to many of their neighbours' homes being torn from their bases and carried away on the floodwaters. They could do nothing but watch, and shiver, and pray. It was to be a very long night not only for the senior Wards, but also for their son Douglas and daughter Greta Ritchie.

Douglas Ward and his wife were returning from a Friday night dance at DeHavilland, where he too worked, when he heard the sound of sirens from the Raymore Drive area. He tried unsuccessfully to get information about his parents, then called Greta, his sister, in the hope that they might be with her. Greta had been watching television unaware of anything more than a bad storm. Now, thoroughly alarmed at her brother's call, she immediately began her own search for information, a search paralleled by thousands of others over the next few hours. Weston police and fire departments were sorry, but could offer little information and even less hope for anyone living on Raymore Drive. They told of efforts to put boats in the water to reach stranded people, where the boats were turned to matchsticks in the pressure of the floodwaters. Struggling to remain calm, think clearly, and if possible, do something constructive, Greta called the Wards' minister, the Reverend Thomas Butler, of St. Matthias Church on Scarlett Road. He had no more knowledge than the police and was just then on his way to the area.

Greta threw on warm clothes and set out to find her mother and father. It was necessary to plead with the officers who were guarding the bridge over the Humber at Bloor Street. They were in the process of closing it, fearing it could collapse (which it did, a short time later), but after hearing Greta's story, they did let her through and she made her way to the Raymore neighbourhood in search of her parents.

She was completely unprepared for the horror she found. Where her parents' home and the homes of their neighbours once stood was now a muddy, churning, fast-flowing river, swollen to at least ten times its normal width. She found her brother working with firemen who were still vainly trying to launch boats. A great knot of fear welled up inside her as she looked at the emptiness where once had been her family home. No one seemed to know anything. It was hard to keep down the panic, to keep out the thoughts of what might have happened to her parents.

Greta joined the army of relatives searching, asking, pleading for information about family members. There were throngs of people in the area: people who had responded to pleas now being broadcast for help; people who had just come to look; and people dislocated by the flood. One man told Greta he didn't know about her parents, but he was rounding up children who were lost and confused. At that point there were fifteen children at his home where his wife was providing milk and cookies and then bedding the youngsters down for the rest of the night. Another gentleman told her he had gone to the Wards' door to warn them of the danger, but her Dad had refused to leave. Another said he had seen her Dad swept away when the water hit the house. Both stories proved erroneous – and tell us much about the rumours that breed on excitement and panic – but at the time they frightened and shook Greta.

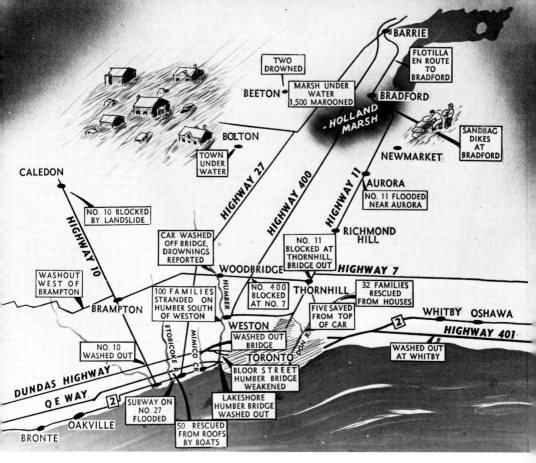

BARRIE

FLOTILLA
EN ROUTE
TO
BRADFORD

TWO
DROWNED

BEETON

MARSH UNDER
WATER
1,500 MAROONED

BRADFORD

HOLLAND
MARSH

BOLTON

TOWN
UNDER
WATER

NEWMARKET

SANDBAG
DIKES
AT
BRADFORD

CALEDON

NO. 10 BLOCKED
BY LANDSLIDE

HIGHWAY 27

HIGHWAY 400

HIGHWAY 11

AURORA

NO. 11 FLOODED
NEAR AURORA

HIGHWAY 10

CAR WASHED
OFF BRIDGE,
DROWNINGS
REPORTED

RICHMOND
HILL

NO. 11
BLOCKED AT
THORNHILL,
BRIDGE OUT

HIGHWAY 7

WOODBRIDGE

WASHOUT
WEST OF
BRAMPTON

100 FAMILIES
STRANDED ON
HUMBER SOUTH
OF WESTON

HUMBER

NO. 400
BLOCKED
AT NO. 7

THORNHILL

32 FAMILIES
RESCUED
FROM HOUSES

BRAMPTON

FIVE SAVED
FROM TOP
OF CAR

WHITBY OSHAWA

HIGHWAY 401

NO. 10
WASHED OUT

ETOBICOKE R.

MIMICO CR.

WESTON

WASHED OUT
BRIDGE

DON R.

WASHED OUT
AT WHITBY

2

TORONTO

BLOOR STREET
HUMBER BRIDGE
WEAKENED

DUNDAS HIGHWAY

Q E WAY

2

SUBWAY ON
NO. 27
FLOODED

LAKESHORE
HUMBER BRIDGE
WASHED OUT

OAKVILLE

BRONTE

50 RESCUED
FROM ROOFS
BY BOATS

This map outlines the extent of the disaster caused by Hurricane Hazel in the part of Ontario surrounding Toronto. *Photo: Toronto Telegram, York University Archives* **(Left)** Hardest hit was the Holland Marsh area, and this photograph shows why witness after witness describes it as "one big lake". *Photo: Toronto Telegram, York University Archives*

It was a cold, blustery day when salvage operations began on the Marsh, hampered by the acres of swept-up vegetables, wooden crates, and other debris—including a little wooden clog. *Photo: Toronto Telegram, York University Archives*

The de Peuter family stands beside the house in which they spent a terrifying night afloat on the Marsh, as described in Harry de Peuter's astonishing story. *Photo: Toronto Star*

On the Holland Marsh, Mr. Auke Ellens' store was left in disarray when the waters receded. *Photos courtesy of Mr. and Mrs. A. Ellens*

The farmers of the Marsh lost no time in returning to their flooded homes in search of anything that could be salvaged. *Photos: Toronto Telegram, Toronto Star*

The clean-up and rescue operation on the Marsh was a sophisticated one involving helicopters and amphibious army vehicles. *Photo: Toronto Telegram, York University Archives*

The plan to pump the Marsh dry was an ambitious one, and Robert Saunders (left) with characteristic energy rushed Ontario Hydro men and equipment to the Marsh. With the help of men like Howard T. Harrison, the Marsh was dry in an incredible twenty-nine days. *Photo: Toronto Star*

In Southampton on Lake Huron, Mrs. Bertha Whittaker was injured when the train she was travelling in toppled off the rain-affected tracks. The engineer and the firemen were trapped in the cab and died of their injuries. *Photos courtesy of Mrs. Howard Gateman*

The International Plowing Match at Brechin was reduced to a flooded shambles that had to be abandoned. *Photos courtesy of S. H. Versteeg*

(Top) Woodbridge, a small community northwest of Toronto, suffered severely. The trailer camp at Pine Grove on the outskirts of the town was devastated. Fortunately, fifteen-year-old Marilyn Norwood was returning to her parents' trailer at midnight in time to see the river overflowing its banks and in time to alert the trailer community. *Photo: Toronto Telegram, York University Archives*   **(Bottom)** *Photo courtesy of J. Ross Jamieson*

(Top) Naval reservists like Sub-lieutenant R. M. Lester (on the running-board of this truck) used whalers to rescue marooned Woodbridge residents and bring them to safety. *Photo courtesy of R. M. Lester* **(Bottom)** In the Woodbridge relief centre, doctors and nurses worked constantly to avert the danger of a typhoid epidemic. Meanwhile, one little child slept peacefully, clutching a toy saved from the flood. *Photo: Toronto Star*

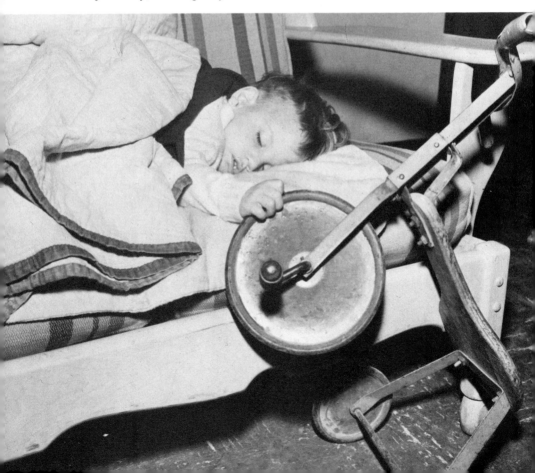

She went from person to person, asking if anyone had seen Mr. and Mrs. Ward of 141 Raymore Drive, and suddenly the man before her was her minister. As gently as he could, he told her of the temporary morgue at the Army-Navy Club near by. She made her way there in terrible fear; then came the relief that brought tears because her parents were not there.

Hours later, as the first streaks of morning lit the sky, the sounds of a helicopter could be heard. A rumour went through the crowd that there were three people on a rooftop and they were alive. Praying that their parents were among the survivors, the young Wards raced up a hill, found the tallest house they could, and without asking anyone's permission, commandeered a ladder and crawled up on the roof. In frustration they found their view was blocked by some large trees and they could only catch glimpses of the helicopter. They decided they would wait until the helicopter had touched down twice at the improvised landing field at a nearby church, and would then go to see if those rescued were Mum and Dad. It was an agony of waiting as they watched the helicopter come back once . . . and then it did not come back again.

They hurried to the landing field just as an ambulance drove away. A neighbour, Mrs. Isherwood, told Greta she thought the gentleman in the ambulance was her father. "The only thing is," she said, "that man had white hair and your Dad's hair isn't white." Police officers at the scene had taken names and Greta, hearing that the people in the ambulance were her mother and father, burst into tears. The officers explained that the ambulance was going to St. Joseph's Hospital.

The journey to the hospital seemed endless – through snarled traffic that hardly moved. So it took some time before the Ward family was reunited in a hospital room.

Greta says she will be eternally grateful to the Sisters and administrative staff at the hospital for their care and concern. The Wards had been put together in one room, made comfortable, given preventive medication, and provided with food and clothing. "Those were pre-OHIP days," Greta points out, "when hospitals normally were reimbursed before patients could go home. The hospital declined to bill us for anything."

Joe and Annie Ward were exhausted from the long, cold ordeal. Happy to see their son and daughter, after the first few explanations and the recounting of the somewhat nerve-wracking helicopter rescue from the rooftop by pilot Bruce Best, they wanted to know from their children if the Raymore Drive house had survived at all, and if they had Lassie, the dog.

"I was twenty-five years old at the time and the hardest thing I ever had to do was say, 'There is nothing left, and we haven't found Lassie,'" Greta remembers.

The Wards went home with Greta and her husband, to stay in their apartment until it could be decided what to do next. Sunday morning, when they went back to see the results of Hurricane Hazel, it was difficult to tell exactly where the house had stood. All the familiar landmarks were missing: the trees, the other houses, the foot bridge. Instead there was rubble, huge slabs of concrete, literally tons of mud and silt and bricks and boards. There was no sign of vegetation. All the gardens and trees were buried or had been washed away.

They did find some of Joe's and Annie's personal possessions. Not much, but they are items still in Joe Ward's possession today. A copper kettle that had been a gift from Annie Ward's mother in England, a little the worse for wear, but still standing on the hearth at Greta's summer home. Oddly, they found the livingroom carpet, three hundred yards downstream. Greta stumbled on it, as it lay buried in silt and muck. Covered with mud, it was terribly heavy, but Joe and his daughter managed to carry it away and have it cleaned. Joe Ward still has it in his present home. The most amazing find of all was the kitchen corner cupboard, standing upright with all the good dishes just where Annie had put them after washing them. Those dishes were and still are the ones the Wards use for holidays and special occasions.

The loss of the dog Lassie was still on the Wards' minds, so much so that several days later Joe spoke of having dreamed of seeing Lassie walking towards him. That same day, Greta received a telephone call from a ham-radio operator who had found Lassie. It was a happy Joe Ward who went off to buy some dog food and retrieve the friendly wire-haired terrier. As nearly as could be pieced together, when the Wards' roof collapsed and made a hole in the Andersons' home, Lassie wound up in the Andersons'. When the water receded the dog was found by searchers curled up on the chesterfield sound asleep. Taken to the church and tied up there, the dog twice chewed through the rope and made her way back to the river. Finally someone recognized her as the Wards' dog and placed the welcome call to Greta Ritchie.

Molly and Jack Anderson, who had left their house during the hurricane, launched their motor boat in an effort to rescue a family across the road from them. Their boat was swamped before they were able to complete the rescue. The Andersons were thrown into the water and swept downstream, surviving only because of the life-jackets they were wearing. Both wound up in the hospital.

When Greta Ritchie called Molly in hospital to ask if there was anything she could do to help her, Molly said she had only one request: "Please tell your mother to leave her house at home next time she comes to call. It made a hell of a hole in the side of ours."

In one duplex on the street there lived ten members of two families: Ken Edwards, his wife Joan, and their three children, Caroline, four, Frank, three, and John, aged three months; and John and Jean Neil, with their three children, Darlene, six, Susan, five, and Adele, three. Ken Edwards and Jean Neil were brother and sister. The Edwards family was a large, closely knit one.

Ken, a fair, quiet, handsome man, was at that time working as an attendant for a service station on Bloor Street West. He had changed jobs a couple of times when firms he worked for had wanted him to go on the road. He was determined not to be away from his young wife and growing family, and was finding the garage work compatible with his own considerable mechanical skills.

Jean Neil, his sister, was married to John "Red" Neil, who worked for General Electric. It had been Jean's idea to rent and share the 148 Raymore Drive property. Jean had always been the girl with energy and ideas. As a youngster she had taken on a paper route just as she had seen her older brother do. She had done some bookkeeping for a neighbourhood doctor, and in the fall of 1954 she was with a real estate firm. It was through her work she heard of the availability of the duplex. With her customary drive and enthusiasm, it was Jean who put through the deal. Because of the pretty location alongside the Humber River, it wasn't too difficult to persuade her brother Ken, with his affection for anything with the look of country or outdoors, to go along. Their respective spouses became as enthusiastic as the brother and sister, and the two couples with their six young children had quickly settled into a pleasant existence in the west-end neighbourhood. They were happy to be there and the house represented something of an achievement for them

– a shared family place and in a picturesque setting. Perfect until such time as each family could afford separate homes and the goal of home ownership.

Friday night, Charles Edwards, Ken and Jean's father, arrived home from his work at Simpson's Appliance Store at Lawrence Plaza, and he and his wife talked about the wild weather and the rains which seemed to grow steadily heavier. Mrs. Edwards, Sr., had been speaking to her son and daughter on the phone, as she did almost every day, and recounted how she had asked if they wanted to come over and stay the night. Jean said, no, they weren't in any danger. Things were all right and John, her husband, had gone to the Veterans' Club, as planned, to attend a stag for a close friend.

As the evening grew later Mrs. Edwards' concern increased. About midnight she phoned her daughter again. Jean said she had just come in the door with her brother Ken, after helping neighbours move furniture from their flooded basement. Mrs. Edwards was about to insist they come for the night when there was a loud noise and Jean said hurriedly she thought it must be Ken moving his car up to higher ground; she would have to go and see. She would call her mother back.

That was the last living contact with any of the nine people in the duplex on Raymore Drive. When John Neil returned to the street at 1:30 a.m. he was met by the extraordinary sight of floodwaters, and the entire street washed away. Thinking his wife and children and the Edwardses were already evacuated, he immediately pitched in with others to help where he could. It was not until the daylight hours that he discovered that his entire family was gone.

It was after 10:00 a.m. when Charles Edwards got word at work that his son Ken, his daughter-in-law Joan, his daughter Jean, and all six of his little grandchildren were lost.

For John Neil there was not only the trauma of an entire family wiped out, but the anguish of being the lone survivor. For Charles Edwards there began a lonely vigil along the riverbanks of the Humber. Every day he walked those riverbanks with a boxer dog by his side, searching for members of his family. He was not the one to find them. The girls' bodies were found first. Ken's body was not found until many days after the hurricane. When Charles learned where his son's body was discovered, he searched downstream from there, reasoning that Ken might well have had a boy in each arm and that they, being lighter, would be swept further downstream. The two little boys were never found.

After the tears and the funeral, Hurricane Hazel was a subject Mrs. Edwards could not bear to hear mentioned. It remained for Charles to deal meticulously with the many small details that are left after a death. How do you react to the correct and proper language of a bank letter telling you they are forwarding you their official cheque for $70.43, the balance at credit in a savings account of your son and daughter-in-law?

The wreck of Ken's car brought an offer of $25 from a salvage company, and a cheque which later bounced. There were matters of life insurance and birth certificates that had to be tendered. There were letters to and from the police itemizing the house contents and similar letters to and from insurance companies. There was correspondence with the Ontario Hurricane Relief Fund, and finally a cheque from the Fund in December to pay the funeral costs for Kenneth, Joan, and Caroline Edwards and Jean, Darlene, Susan, and Adele Neil. The cheque was for $1,328.73.

Twenty-five years later Mr. Charles Edwards has not only all the newspaper clippings that tell the story of Hazel, but also a binder full of all the merciless bits of paper that use flat, cold words to tell what no words can convey. Miraculously the elder Edwards is a man of no bitterness. He has been able to come to terms with the enormous loss, and did so at the time. The pain will never go, but there has never been any bitterness. He is able to speak gratefully of his employers, who were considerate and helpful to him at the time, and those comments are in his own written account of the events.

When asked about John Neil, his son-in-law, the only survivor of 148 Raymore Drive, he says sadly that they used to see him a great deal at first. After a time the visits grew less frequent. For a time there were exchanged Christmas cards. Now, no contact at all. He thinks John has remarried and built his life over again. There is not the slightest hint of criticism in his comments. He gives the impression that this indeed is as it should be.

The Keller family were double losers in the hurricane flood. They were scheduled to move from their temporary home on Raymore to a permanent one, also on Raymore. By morning, neither existed. They had no insurance.

For those who did escape there were frantic seconds of grabbing precious possessions. The choices made by some are interesting; one woman managed to save her budgies; someone else a cat; another an elderly pet dog; another, a Bible and an old family picture.

On the morning of Saturday, October 16, Raymore Drive, once a quiet, pleasant little street, was a scene of bleak desolation. A few trees jutted forlornly out of the water at grotesque angles and on the east side of the river were tons of stones, rocks, boulders, debris, and pieces of houses brought down by the floodwaters. Thirty-six people were dead, sixty families were homeless, and twelve hundred feet of the street was simply gone. It was the worst single event of the hurricane passing in Ontario.

Weary rescue workers made their headquarters at a little church around the corner from Raymore Drive. There, survivors sat silent, staring into space as though the whole night were too much to comprehend. Tom McGarvey, the man who had been tied to a tree to prevent him from trying a suicidal rescue, could not speak to his son, young Tom, when they met. What do you say when you know seventeen-year-old Donald is dead and Mrs. McGarvey and daughter Jacqueline are on the list of missing, believed dead?

Incredibly, the whole catastrophe of Raymore Drive had lasted not much more than an hour. In that hour the river had risen more than twenty feet. By the end of the hour the screams had stopped. Those stranded had either been rescued, or could see rescue coming . . . or they had been washed away in the flood.

Perhaps the last word about Raymore Drive should be this. Lotta Dempsey was a veteran journalist, a woman who had travelled much of the world, reporting all manner of stories – a thorough professional. *Globe and Mail* City Editor Turnbull remembers Lotta Dempsey calling in her story of Raymore Drive. She was sobbing.

CHAPTER ELEVEN

AFTERMATH

Saturday morning, October 16, 1954, saw the last of Hurricane Hazel, and a sleepy Toronto wakened to the sight of disaster such as it had never known. The creeks and rivers that had surged through its sleeping villages had left a trail of carnage and tangled wreckage it would take years to erase from some areas. For people in places not hit by the hurricane there was incredulity as radio reports began telling of the damage and loss of life. People simply could not believe that this had happened here, only a mile or two away from where they slept soundly in their beds. It seemed literally incredible, and to many it still does.

J. C. Fraser, a teacher at Lawrence Park Collegiate, was among those who could not believe the damage: "The old iron Hogg's Hollow bridge on Yonge Street was washed out, and for months afterwards we had to negotiate a Bailey over the Don. It was sad but also comical to see the houses which had been built on the edge of the Don, where it takes a bend just before the bridge, projecting out over the river. The force of the water at the bend had washed away the bank and these houses lost their whole front lawn and the earth under them so that the house was sticking out from the bank about eight to ten feet. There are no houses there today.

"The water carried this mud into the low-lying houses in Hogg's Hollow on the east side of Yonge St. The water literally flowed in the back door and out the front door of many of them and I remember seeing the people shovelling away the mud which was about a foot deep and flowed like a river through the house and out the front door."

The slow business of taking stock, counting casualties, trying to discover who had been lost, began at once. In the early stages on Saturday, information was sketchy, hard to put together. And as people heard the news they complicated matters by taking to the roads to see for themselves. Marcel Cox, the Commissioner of Roads and Sanitation for Etobicoke, was so exasperated by what he calls "sightseers and ghoulish people" that he ordered the bridge over the Humber at Lambton closed with barricades. Then he carried on with his work, going forty-eight straight hours without sleep.

Mrs. Mary B. Collins, a volunteer driver for the Red Cross, was just one of an army of volunteers of that organization who pitched in to help with the job of matching up missing persons, reuniting families, locating relatives, working out of local church halls and many hastily improvised headquarters. In the Red Cross cafeteria, even CNIB volunteers did their bit, working round the clock to provide hot drinks and what comfort they could.

The Red Cross, in fact, was involved from the start. At 10:30 on the night of the storm they were contacted by the Long Branch police asking if they could send blankets and assistance. A Toronto branch officer promptly gathered a team of volunteers together, and before midnight two trucks, a private car, and a police escort were speeding towards the disaster area. That was the beginning of the Red Cross effort, which would total 20,000 miles driven and 28,000 hours worked, an average of 175 hours per member. Setting up registries in all the localities hit by Hazel, and then forwarding them to a central registry, was one monumental job done by these volunteers. The central registry, worked round the clock the first few days, compiling lists of families for the purpose of inquiry and assistance. Food, clothing, and medical assistance were provided.

One of the most unpleasant but most essential services was the provision of an emergency morgue. J. R. McFadden, along with Elliot Baker, found himself involved in that task. On the Saturday morning he and some friends were driving towards the Humber: "A voice on the car radio was asking for volunteers to go to the Etobicoke Police Station. As soon as we stepped into the line for volunteers we were selected out of the line and taken to the Coroner's office. My friend was wearing a medical jacket from the U. of T., and was asked if he was in Medical School and if he had done his work on cadavers yet. His positive response evoked a request from the Coroner and the Chief of Police, Andy Hamilton, that we set up a central morgue on the second floor of the old Fire Department, on the north side of Dundas Street just west of Burnhamthorpe Road.

"The second floor was roughly divided down the middle by portable dividers. The entrance, which was at the back, was to be used for incoming and outgoing bodies, as well as those people coming to try and identify their loved ones. As you entered the area, the Salvation Army people were doing an outstanding job of assisting the distraught people in search of their loved ones. Behind the partition, the now Dr. Elliot Baker and I were accepting the incoming bodies. Our job of setting up and administrating the morgue turned out to be one of cleaning the bodies as best we could and searching for some identification. We would then write a brief description of the body and where it was found, tag the toe, and give the description to the Salvation Army. Here, behind the partition, we had three rows of bodies, men, women, and children in order of age. Each body was covered with a blanket.

"It was obvious to us that many of these people had been swept away in the night as they were still in their pyjamas, and apparently had no chance at all of surviving.

"Our most upsetting experience was seeing one of our former public-school janitors, a volunteer fireman, brought in after having been killed trying to save the lives of others. We had known this man well and admired him for many years. We knew well his involvement with the volunteer fire department, as many times when the old firebell behind the school would ring we would see him run across the school yard to fulfil his obligation.

"I remember one kind gentleman who came in to identify an old retired employee who had no family and had lived on Raymore Drive. The employer simply wanted to give his former friend a dignified burial.

"I have often wondered how many of those ill-fated people might have survived if they had not gone back to gather up some personal possession which some of them were still clutching."

Dorothy Anderson was a Red Cross worker who helped in the morgue. Her job was "to aid and feed the people who came to identify the bodies brought there, loved ones killed in the hurricane.

"I remember long lines of tables where bottles of aspirin sat – the only thing we had to offer these poor souls to help them in a time of distress. That and the tea and coffee we served endlessly."

Mrs. Anderson remembers encountering one "very

pale-faced girl" among her co-workers and discovering
on inquiry that she "had volunteered to wash the faces of
the dead before the relatives saw them, as they were covered in mud from the river." She remembers the smell of
burning blankets, destroyed after bringing in a body, and
remembers the people who came in to view the dead,
seeking – yet dreading to find – a loved one. She remembers "the young man who waited for three days. He had
lost all of a family of eight. And the young boy who had
gone to a show in Weston and could not get back over the
river to his mother and dad, who were swept away in the
flood. He kept saying he could have saved them."

While the Red Cross and the Salvation Army did
yeoman work indoors, the military were called in to help
in the clean-up outside. In the course of his army career
Fred Kelly had been involved in fighting the great Win-
nipeg flood of 1950, so he knew about the destruction
wrought by water on the rampage. When Hazel hit Toronto he, along with two hundred of his colleagues, was
sent from Camp Borden to assist people to save their be-
longings, and also to try to find bodies lost in the floods:
"I was an Acting Sergeant at the time and my crew of
men and I were assigned to patrol the area where the old
Queensbury Hotel used to be. We had about one-half
mile above and below the hotel, including the Lambton
Golf and Country Club. I can remember finding two
bodies when we were working with pike poles dragging
the river." Fred Kelly's work held special terrors, for he
knew that his sixteen-year-old brother was among those
drowned.

Jack Bullions was with the Navy Militia from H.M.C.S.
York who went to Ashbridge's Bay to pick up whalers
from the Sea Cadet Corps and take them up to the Holland Marsh to help in rescue operations. From Camp
Borden the Army brought "Ducks", motor vehicles

which could also travel in water. Jack Bullions, with others, worked most of the night and on Saturday scoured the Humber Valley, retrieving the bodies of victims and also the carcasses of dogs, cats, and livestock. The grim work remains a vivid memory for him. He remembers pulling in the body of one man whose hand still held, in a death grip, a piece of a child's tartan skirt, mute testimony to a failed rescue attempt.

One young Boy Scout who was working with him in the aftermath of the storm helped pull in the body of a man, only to turn it over and discover it was his father. "It was an awful shock to the boy," Bullions says, shaking his head sadly. "It was just terrible. There's nothing else to say about it. It was just terrible."

Police, firemen, Boy Scouts, Red Cross, the military, all pitched in to help where they could at disaster areas along the flooded river and creeks. One field operation was set up opposite where Scarlett Wood Court is today. From this base and others like it, trucks, cruisers, and manpower were able to operate. While these organizations did magnificent work in those terrible hours, among the unsung heroes of Hurricane Hazel are the many individuals like Vernon Maguire, a truck driver for the CPR, who on Saturday told his wife that he was going to see if he could be of any help.

When he got to the Humber he began to search the river: "I noticed what I thought was a teddy bear half buried in the mud, probably thrown there during the height of the storm. I waded out in the mud and discovered I had found the small body of a boy around six or seven years of age. Picking up the body I found that I was firmly stuck in the mud and afraid to turn around without possibly falling. Hearing someone behind me I turned my upper body around and handed the little boy to a man who I believe was a fireman.

"I worked myself free, returned to shore, and left immediately. I walked all the way home, cold, wet, and sick."

Gail Palmer, a reporter for the *Telegram*, had a similar experience. She waded in waist deep to pick up what she thought was a doll, only to find she had picked up a little baby. Thereafter she made her way to H. H. Fuller's store, so upset she had to lie down.

Maryon Kushner, then a little girl of eleven, was standing with her family by the Etobicoke Creek mouth, gazing out at the lake where partly submerged trailers bobbed like traffic buoys. "A large house trailer floated past and unexpectedly overturned, exposing a body that was caught under the wreckage. We all stood helpless."

Further north a small boy was witnessing an equally frightening sight: Dave Sanderson was only eight, and he and his brother considered the whole thing "a big adventure" and were up early that Saturday morning to see the Eglinton Flats at the end of their street. "And then we quickly learned what a disaster was. The sight in the valley was indescribable – it was a *lake* with water midway up the windows of the houses! We could see people on the roofs of several houses, huddled under blankets for warmth, but there was little anyone could do but watch because there were no boats.

"There were about 150 of us looking at this disaster, and I remember we could hear people shouting back and forth to those on the roofs, many of whom had been out there most of the night and were suffering from exposure.

"One group seemed to be hysterical, doing lots of screaming and crying and running about on the roof. We learned later it was because somebody had drowned, and was bobbing around in the water inside the house.

"It seemed the longer we all stood there doing nothing, the more upset we all became looking at these poor folks in the valley."

Dave Sanderson's father was one of the thousands of men and women involved in working night and day to clear up in the wake of Hazel. Mr. Sanderson, who was with Toronto Hydro, worked for thirty-six straight hours trying to restore power. Bill Swann, the Borough of Etobicoke's engineer, was involved in rounding up supplies, pumps, ropes, and, in the pre-dawn hours, floodlights – all the paraphernalia of emergencies. Since he was responsible for the design, construction, and operation of roads, bridges, and sewers in Etobicoke, Bill Swann worked seventy-two consecutive hours without sleep. For the first forty-eight hours the entire municipality virtually operated out of his office.

E. R. Dent was another of the army of men and women who worked without sleep. His job was to fix the pumps on the Old Mill pumping station, a job made hideous by the fact that the sewage from the area had overflowed and was being discharged around him and his three colleagues.

"You can imagine our physical condition, despite coveralls, and rubber boots, etc. *Everything* was covered in mud and sewage. We did not sleep, or rest, or go home – we worked right through the Saturday night, and thanks to the Red Cross for the Mobile Canteen, to the army for portable lights, and to terrific support from our boss, we managed to have things working sometime on Sunday. We were tired, smelly, dirty, and hungry, but our job was done, the water diverted, and rescue operations could begin.

"Then – the most wonderful thing happened. Our boss appeared on the scene and promptly marched these four foul-smelling electricians, coveralls, rubber boots, and all, into the very elegant Old Mill Restaurant on Sunday afternoon, and bought us the most wonderful hot dinner. After thirty-six hours' straight work, he thought we deserved this surprise. In our eyes he was twelve feet tall that day."

Meanwhile, according to Helen MacNeil who worked at the Bell Telephone Company, the situation was hectic and confused there. Many of the girls stayed right at the office and did not get home for a week, working long hours and double shifts. With the phones jammed with overwork, communications were in a desperate state. In these circumstances, press, radio stations, and radio hams, all offered every assistance they could. Even manufacturers of communications equipment – Rogers Majestic Electronics, Canadian General Electric, Canadian Marconi, Canadian Westinghouse, and Pye Canada Limited – worked together to set up a special hook-up, "Manufacturers' Network", covering Woodbridge, Bradford, Etobicoke, Weston, and Thistletown. With 25,000 calls at the Red Cross switchboard in less than forty-eight hours, the need for all help possible was obvious. With eleven new direct lines and five extensions promptly installed by Bell Telephone, and an elaborate system of networks and connecting channels, communication was gradually established with all emergency points. Mobile units, walkie-talkie hand sets, public address systems, and jeep units were all used, and eighty-two members of the Amateur Radio Emergency Corps worked from twenty-eight mobile units. Among them was Cyril Cole of Hamilton, who notes that "several carloads of equipment and operators" went from that city to help their neighbours. Cole himself was assigned to Woodbridge and then Malton airport, co-ordinating a shuttle air service between Malton and Downsview. He still remembers the shock on the faces of people wandering around trying to find "a place to start to just do something!"

On Saturday, rescue operations and surveying of

damages involved the extensive use of helicopters. Premier Leslie Frost himself telephoned Upper Canada College to request landing privileges on the playing fields for government helicopters. Unfortunately the call was answered by a new secretary just out from England, and the following conversation took place:

PREMIER FROST:	"I wish to speak to the Principal. Premier Frost calling."
SECRETARY:	"I'm sorry this is not the right number. I will put you through to the lady dietitian who deals with refrigeration problems."

Mary Sowby, wife of the then principal, Dr. C. W. Sowby, recounts that Premier Frost dined out on this story many times. One amusing note on an otherwise sad day.

Elizabeth Fowler needed no reminder of the day's sadness. She lived on Scarlett Road, about half a mile south of Raymore Drive, and had spent a long, anxious night when the family had responded to a past-midnight alarm to leave their house. Returning to her home the next day, she was shocked to look out the back window and see the body of a man caught in a tree. Rescue workers came along and carried him away, and Miss Fowler learned he had been a resident of Raymore Drive.

By contrast, among the clean-up crews was a group of volunteers from the University of Toronto's engineering department. Don Jackson was among the students who worked on the Humber Valley just south of the present 401 highway. He recalls that because a balloon factory had been flooded out upstream, hundred of balloons were strewn on the ground and hanging from trees. Obviously a golf course had been hit, too, because high in a tree stood a sign warning, "Players please replace divots."

There was much that was admirable and even heroic in the reaction showed by ordinary people in the wake of the storm. Sadly, there was much that was despicable, too. The morbid curiosity of sightseers that hampered rescue work was bad enough. Worse, looters made their hideous appearance; some flooded-out families carefully brought their most cherished possessions to dry land, only to have them stolen. Ghouls, people who searched for bodies to rob them of any jewellery or valuables, made their appearance, too. To counter this, squads of police, RCAF, Navy Guards, and twenty RCMP officers were rushed into the flood-ravaged areas of Thistletown, Woodbridge, and North York.

Frank and Mary Wakeman of Weston encountered looters, too, after going through a terrible time during the flood, when they sat upstairs clutching their two-year-old and listening to "debris and other houses banging into our house", before finally being rescued by boat, "the last to be rescued in the valley". For them the aftermath of the storm was a strange mixture of experiences: "When the waters receded, we went to look at our home that had been paid for just two weeks prior to this. There was a telephone pole through our front window, golf clubs on the table inside, and various pieces of silver and china scattered throughout the house – none of which were ours. On our front lawn was a two-storey house broken in half." The Wakemans were left with what was on their backs, little more, and were "thoroughly overwhelmed at the generosity and kindness of neighbours and strangers alike." Yet when the police guard on the house was withdrawn, "the looters came in full force, taking everything salvageable, even to digging the flowers out of the gardens."

There were profiteers, too. Jack Bullions, assigned to the Woodbridge area with the Navy rescue and clean-up squads, remembers a coffee wagon coming around. Weary volunteers flocked to it, only to find that the vendor wanted fifty cents for a cup of coffee and a dollar for a hot dog, scandalous prices for 1954. The enterprising vendor got what he deserved. The police moved in fast, took the fellow over to their cruiser for a little chat, and told the volunteers to help themselves to what they wanted. Which they did, displaying good, hearty appetites.

That Saturday the *Globe and Mail* headlined the story: "Great Storm Hits after 4-inch Rain – Winds 70, Dykes Fail, Motorists in Trees". Even then the full impact of Hurricane Hazel was not known. It would take several days before the death toll could be taken with anything like accuracy, and missing persons located. It was almost as though no one could, or would, believe that such a catastrophe could happen here.

In the days that followed the count came in: eighty-one dead; thirty-six on one street alone, Raymore Drive; other victims in Woodbridge, New Toronto, Islington, Beeton, Thistletown. In the Holland Marsh area alone, three thousand homeless; on Raymore Drive sixty homeless; seven hundred in Woodbridge; at Highland Creek another sixty families with homes gone. The dollar value of damage was difficult to estimate, but figures ran anywhere from $25 million to many times that.

Dollars were not in many minds as people read the Dead and Missing list in that morning's *Globe and Mail*: "Bruce Lanning, 10, 324 Leslie Street, Oshawa, drowned near Unionville when swept from his father's shoulders; Stewart Nicholson, Palmerston CNR Fireman, killed in derailment at Southampton; Edward Albert Jeffries, 69, drowned at Etobicoke; Mrs. Annie Curtis, Long Branch, drowned when home swept away; George Summers, Deseronto, killed in car accident during the storm; J. T. Henderson, Selby, killed in car accident during the storm." On and on the list read, its flat, brief phrases telling the night's horror story perhaps more effectively than volumes of dramatic prose.

On that Saturday morning only four of the twenty-eight bridges within the townships' boundaries were operative. Some bridges washed out; others had their approaches eroded away; and still others gave way under the mountainous pressure of debris piled against abutments and approaches. Bill Swann, still at his desk, co-ordinated the job of assessing the damages and ordering trucks with crushed stone and fill from quarries out at Milton to get rolling.

When the news of the Hurricane Hazel disaster reached Montreal, Molson's Brewery Limited quickly made arrangements to dispatch their large "Mobile Emergency Unit" to Toronto. The Emergency Unit was about 60 feet long and over two feet wider than a regular transport van, and as a result it was necessary to have the Provincial Police escort the unit the entire distance.

Robert R. Swan remembers: "The unit was divided into a rest area, a large medical and first aid area with fully equipped operating room, a radio room with a very modern and powerful two-way radio set with a generator to supply power to operate it at all times, and a small kitchen to supply a refreshment counter that opened out across the back of the van. There was a supply of powerful search lights, loud speakers, walkie-talkies, stretchers, blankets, and other emergency equipment available.

"The unit arrived in Toronto on the Sunday following the disaster and was in service for about two weeks in the area east of the Humber River between Toronto and Bradford. The radio was in operation twenty-four hours a day assisting the authorities in locating residents who had left or lost their homes. The coffee, tea, and food service (compliments of Molson's) was greatly appreciated by the many volunteers who worked long hours searching for survivors buried in the debris and locating bodies. The medical room staffed by two nurses gave aid and comfort to the injured, but the big job was the inoculation of hundreds of residents against typhoid when there was danger of the water supply becoming contaminated." During the two weeks following the disaster, the Molson's Mobile Emergency Unit and its staff continued to supply a 24-hour service in the stricken area.

In the Monday, October 18, edition of the *Toronto Daily Star*, Gordon Sinclair's readers found him writing about the major Toronto news story of the year from a distance of five hundred miles. He was in New York as part of his show-biz beat. He recalls that he found it pretty spooky to be sitting in a hotel room, six storeys above Times Square, watching on TV the churning waters of the Don, on whose banks he was born, and the Mimico Creek, on whose banks he now lived, rolling and boiling at full flood, and then headlines from the *Star*, for which he had worked for thirty-three years, marching across the screen there in New York. He told his readers how the *Star*'s headlines and photographs had blazed across TV screens, telling millions of Americans of the hurricane and its toll of people and property in Southern Ontario. By comparison, he said, the Jackie Gleason show, which he reviewed, seemed very pallid.

Toronto's Hurricane Hazel ordeal hit the front page of the *New York Times* and was big news all across the world. In Nice, France, Daphne Straumann was checking into a hotel: "The clerk looked up from my registration card and said, 'Oh, your town has been wiped out.' When I asked what he meant, he said, 'A hurricane has hit Toronto and wiped it out.' My first thought was, 'This is impossible,' and I didn't believe the clerk."

At home and abroad generous-hearted citizens promptly met the emergency with the only practical help they could give – cash.

Ken Armstrong, then with MacLaren Advertising Company, found himself heavily involved in that process. The Monday following Hazel's arrival he was asked to report to Premier Frost's office, where he found himself in a group including Colonel Eric Phillips, a Toronto industrialist, Neil J. MacKinnon, then General Manager of the Canadian Bank of Commerce, Beland Honderich of the *Toronto Daily Star*, and Don Henshaw of MacLaren's. In the course of a short meeting Colonel Phillips was named Chairman of the Hurricane Hazel Relief Fund, Neil MacKinnon became Treasurer, and Ken Armstrong (who had been tipped off earlier) was made Public Relations Director. At that Queen's Park meeting Beland Honderich made the first official contribution to the fund, $250,000 on behalf of the Atkinson Charitable Foundation.

Ken Armstrong continues: "Following the meeting I spent some time with Mr. Frost, who had obviously been deeply moved by the disaster. I suggested that he make a helicopter trip over the flooded area, which was quickly arranged. . . . On the following afternoon, October 19, an organization meeting of the Flood Relief Fund was held in the King Edward Hotel, and chaired by Fred 'Big Daddy' Gardiner. A broad cross-section of Ontario leaders in commerce, industry, politics, and organized labour attended. At one point a leading Toronto businessman, who shall remain nameless, inquired as to whether funds would be made available to restore the greens of his golf club.

"Fred Gardiner reacted like a bull gone berserk. Not one penny would be spent on such frivolous nonsense, he said. The fund would be used to restore the shattered lives of those who had lost family and property to the floods.

"As soon as the public became aware of the address of the Relief Fund we were inundated by mail contributions. Six to fifteen bags of mail were arriving three times a day. . . . I recall that George Burt, leader of the UAW, dropped in quite informally to present us with a cheque for $10,000. Corporations large and small were making generous contributions, but it was the small donations from widows, the elderly, and schoolchildren that really warmed our hearts." A flow of money that quickly neared the million-dollar mark came rushing in from a sympathetic and public-spirited citizenry all across Canada, and even from other parts of the world. From the Pope there was a $10,000 donation, announced by James Cardinal McGuigan; from Hamilton citizens and business firms, $100,000; and from the B.C. Flood Emergency Fund, $100,000. They knew all about floods out there. Their Fund had been set up during the Fraser Valley disaster of 1948.

But the size of the donation did not always tell the whole story. From Edward C. Ward, a newcomer to the country, came his full pay cheque as an employee of Kresge's warehouse. In his letter accompanying the cheque, Mr. Ward explained he had met kindness and friendliness. This was his small way of giving thanks, and rendering help to the victims of the hurricane.

The Hurricane Hazel Relief Fund was a wonderful success. Ken Armstrong remembers seeing the final financial statements; after all needs had been filled "only a few thousand dollars remained in the kitty. Mr. Mac-Kinnon, the canny banker, had balanced his books."

Governor General Vincent Massey, Premier Leslie Frost, and Metro Chairman Fred Gardiner, all made tours of the worst scenes of devastation. Premier Frost pledged $100,000 immediate credit for the farmers of the Holland Marsh. The damage to what had been a piece of Canada's richest farm land was already being estimated at $10 million. In Ottawa, Prime Minister Louis St. Laurent met with Finance Minister Harris, and it was announced that there would be immediate federal help forthcoming.

One consequence of the hurricane that seemed particularly incongruous was a great round of criticism directed towards the Queen and the United Kingdom, who had not sent any aid, not even a telegram of sympathy. Front-page stories told of flustered Canadian officials in London and their mumbled stories about currency regulations that would hamper money donations, and supplies that would be too late in arriving to be really useful. Absolutely idiotic statements were made to the effect that the official line was that Hurricane Hazel was a grade-B catastrophe, unworthy of overseas recognition. An anonymous spokesman at Canada House in London was credited with that gem, which must have made strange reading for any of Hazel's victims in Toronto.

When the smoke had cleared, it became abundantly clear that no personal message had come from Her Majesty because neither the federal government nor the Governor General's Office had provided any information sufficient to warrant one. In fact, the Queen Mother, who was about to embark on a Canada–U.S. tour, had asked for details and, when only sketchy reports were available from Canadian officialdom, had made a point of asking that particulars be sent to her.

The interest and concern of Britons, many of whom had friends and relatives in Ontario, were amply demonstrated by the more than one thousand inquiries at Ontario House in only a few days. Knowledgeable observers were pretty blunt in saying that criticism should more properly be directed to Ottawa, which had given the impression that expressions of sympathy were unnecessary. For the families of the eighty-one persons who lost their lives, such fine points of official protocol must have seemed terribly remote.

When the damages were finally tallied by the Carswell-Shaw Commission, the estimate was $24 million; a far cry from first estimates which went as high as $100 million in the early morning hours of the disaster, but still an appalling total in 1954. Personal property loss was appraised at $6.4 million. Flood damage to Metro-owned property was $2,756,000, most of it for repairs to roads and bridges.

A newly formed Hurricane Homes and Buildings Assistance Board, headed by Norman Long, had the difficult task of dealing with mortgages on an individual basis. It was made clear that the assistance program was designed to help victims rehabilitate themselves and their families, and that efforts would be made to reach settlements that would give something to the mortgager and the mortgagee.

The long-lasting effects of any major disaster are made up of just such details as these. Loss of life and loss of property are the first blows; the long, slow, inexorable business of winding up all the details comes after, and sometimes seems to go on forever. In the minds of many of those whose lives were affected by Hurricane Hazel, it did go on forever.

One postscript will serve as a reminder of that fact. In the summer of 1978, Janet Banaszuk was looking for fossils on the Humber. She found a large rusted axe, which her husband spent hours cleaning, to find it was a fireman's axe. They took it to the Fire Hall on Prince Edward Drive and later heard that their suspicions were correct. The axe had belonged to one of the firemen who died in the river the night that Hurricane Hazel besieged Toronto.

CHAPTER TWELVE

A FAMILY'S DIARY

When a major calamity like Hurricane Hazel occurs, it becomes a media event. Newspaper, radio, and TV tell the myriad details for days, as piece by piece the story unfolds. And then the story is replaced in the news by some other event that captures people's interest. Gradually the disaster story fades from the consciousness of those who were unaffected by it.

But for others, the aftermath is long, tedious, and exhausting. For the thousands of people bereaved or made homeless or in some way harmed by Hurricane Hazel, the storm was not easily forgotten, as this chapter will show.

Mrs. Roy Patrick (Margie) has kept a diary for many years. Her entries over the Hazel period and afterwards are more graphic than any news story.

Oct. 14, 1954.
It's raining again today and the children, Larry (3½), Karen (2) and William (8 months) are in. The house is a wreck but they're happy.
Oct. 15.
Nothing but rain all day. The cellar is getting full and

our sump pump isn't working. Larry said, "The sky is having a big doo all over the place." Hurricane Hazel will arrive at midnight. Roy drove Mr. Jeffries home from work as usual. He's not going to the [Army-Navy] Club tonight.

Sat. Oct. 16.

Evacuated house, came to Doreen's [sister]. Almost got drowned, car and all. Hurricane Hazel came. Seventeen houses on our street are gone. 37 of our neighbours are gone too. Dear God what a tragedy. Last night Chet Swales and the other neighbours were driving up yelling and honking horns, telling people to get out. We couldn't believe there was any danger. But I called the police just to make sure. They told us to get out fast, so in ten minutes we were gone in the car, with the kids in their pyjamas. We took nothing. The lights from the cars lit everything up. The foot bridge was breaking from the weight of debris against it. The waves were awful high. The people around the bend didn't listen, or couldn't hear the warnings. Poor souls. They never had a chance when the huge wave came down. When I think of the disaster it could have been for us, I shiver.

[The next few days' entries chronicle many of the deaths of neighbours and recollections of the Patricks' seven years on Gilhaven. Then:]

Oct. 20.

Everyone is sick with colds. Larry's fever went up so high he had convulsions. That's scary. We are very crowded here and Doreen is expecting. She is sick a lot. We can't stay here. God I'm tired. There's nothing definite about our house. We are told we can't go back.

Oct. 21.

Rev. Butler told me he talked to the Reeve of Etobicoke

last night and they decided we should all have new homes. Seems too good to be true. Everyone has been so good to us. Roy and I are going to register in the township offices. They say for a new house. I still can't believe it. Hurricane Irene is on her way, from the same place Hazel started. My darling Larry is better today. We are all feeling better.

Oct. 22.

We registered and now we wait. There are only six houses they aren't sure of condemning. Ours is the sixth house down. We won't know for two weeks. Roy wants to go back to the house. But it's like death valley to me.

Oct. 23.

Roy has gone to the house today with Benny [Doreen's husband]. We went to Humber Heights school today to register again. I don't know what for. Hurricane Irene fizzled out. She needed to. The Junior Red Cross phoned us and they have new clothes for the children. Wonderful.

Oct. 24.

Today was quiet, although people are still phoning to see if there is anything they can do. I wish I knew where we are going. It's so hard on everyone. Poor Doreen. It's her first baby. She doesn't need us here. Poor Karen too. It's her birthday and I can't have the little party I planned for her.

Oct. 25.

Roy and Ben went coon hunting again. Caught one. Any money he can make will help. He's tired, poor guy. Rev. Butler took us to the church today and gave us outfits from the Red Cross, two big baskets of food, and a cheque for $25. I cried. He's a good man.

Tues., Wed., Thurs., Friday, Sat., Oct. 30.

Scrambled up week. We went to a meeting one night and they told us we could rent a house if we can find one and charge the rent to them. We found one. But they wanted us to sign a lease. We can't do that. The government was to decide today, but we didn't hear anything. It's awful to have no home. I guess I was spoiled. Roy wants to go home. He's at the breaking point. I don't really want to go back, but if he wants to go, I'll go. The place down there looks awful and I worry about the kids getting hurt. Roy has started to get things cleaned up.

Today a big box came from Eaton's and to my delighted surprise, more new clothes for the children. Snow suits, mitts, overshoes, underwear, diapers, plastic pants, baby's blanket, dresses for Karen, blouses, slips, pyjamas. I was real happy. I also had a voucher for $7.50 for frozen foods. They gave me $11.50 worth. Wonderful people!

Oct. 31.

I'm so tired. Maybe it's indigestion in my chest. Worked hard all day, washing walls. [Later she was to have open-heart surgery.]

Nov. 1.

Had the doctor and I am ordered to rest.

Nov. 2.

It's a lot for Doreen in her condition. Roy is getting furniture back into our condemned home. He's determined to get back. The doctor came and told me I have to stay in bed for another week. Ha! Roy went to the Club. He met Ron there. Young Brian is sick and had to have the doctor. They were telling each other all their troubles. They had quite a gab. They don't have much to say to one another as a rule.

Nov. 4.

Doctor came again and gave me hell for getting out of bed. It's impossible. Cecil has been giving William his morning bottle and breakfast. He helps a lot. The township paid Ben and Doreen $30 to help feed us. We can't stay here though.

They are not giving us permission to go back. Linda had Larry for a few days. I miss him terribly.

Nov. 6.

Last night Larry came home and as soon as he saw me he cried. Tonight we all came home. They couldn't keep us out. The sign is still on the door. I don't care. It is good to be home. Everyone worked hard cleaning and washing the house. Linda helped a lot there.

Nov. 7.

Cousin Bruce and June came to stay and help me. I feel so good. Now maybe I can rest. The doctor says another month and I should be well enough for x-rays. I don't want an operation.

Dec. 15.

Long time since I've written in here. We now know our fate. The government is expropriating our property. They are paying us 80 per cent of what they value the place at. The real estate man was here on Monday. He works for the government. He asked me what I thought the place was worth and I said $10,000 and it is. We are going to be in the hole. Our mortgage was being paid for by our tenants upstairs.

Dec. 29.

We had a good Christmas.

Jan. 7, 1955.

Roy filled in his VLA papers tonight. We went to the meeting last night and all turned out well. They said they'd let us know for sure what we'll get by the end of the month. It is rumoured we might have to pay back the $100 we received from the Hurricane Relief Fund. We don't. So that's good.

Feb. 18.

We have had a lot of sickness since we came back into the house and now my darling Karen is in the hospital. They gave her needles of intravenus and she screamed

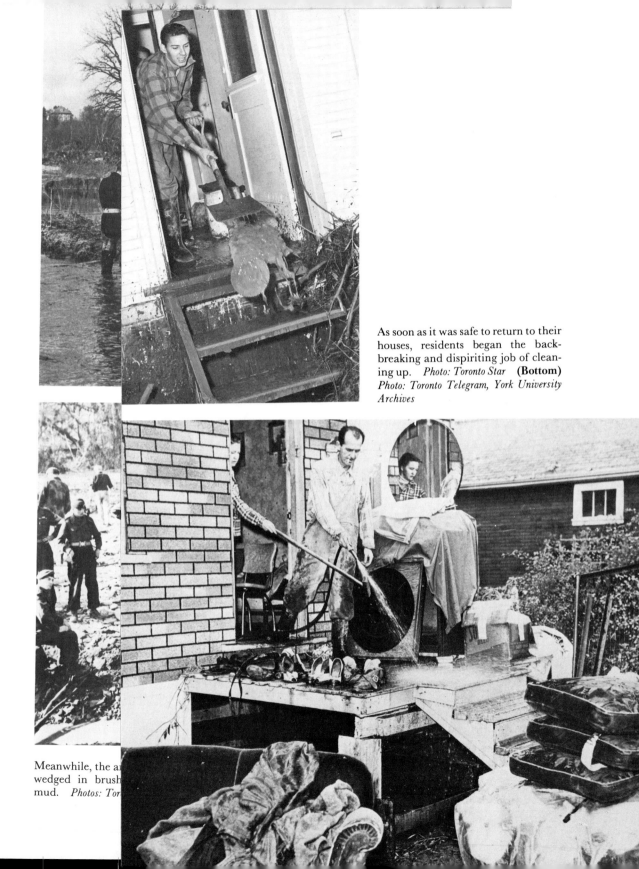

As soon as it was safe to return to their houses, residents began the back-breaking and dispiriting job of cleaning up. *Photo: Toronto Star* **(Bottom)** *Photo: Toronto Telegram, York University Archives*

Meanwhile, the a
wedged in brush
mud. *Photos: Tor*

As word of the [...]
butions to hel[...]
the flood car[...]
concerned citi[...]
Armouries o[...]
Photos: Toronto [...]
Archives

Working south to the lake, the army cleared away the tangled mass of debris, blasting it with flame-throwers or burning it up in enormous bon-fires. *Photo: Toronto Star* **(Bottom)** *Photos: Toronto Telegram, York University Archives*

The storm played havoc with roads and bridges all over the Toronto area. *Photos courtesy of (clockwise): Frank W. Roberts, Mike Filey, Toronto Telegram, J. Edgar Parsons*

The storm left many objects in almost unrecognizable condition.   *Photos: Toronto Telegram, York University Archives*

This view of the Humber River south of the St. Philip's Road bridge demonstrates dramatically how far the Humber exceeded its normal bounds. The lower photograph was taken from the same spot three days later. *Photos courtesy of J. Edgar Parsons*

5 FIREMEN DIED FOR US
5 FAMILIES NEED OUR HELP
give GENEROUSLY !

(Top) A reminder of the tragic effects of Hurricane Hazel.   *Photo: Toronto Star*   (Bottom) Some of the hurricane's effects were more fortunate. The establishment of the Metro Conservation Authority meant that the flood plains were protected and turned into delightful parks. This 1979 scene makes the twelve-foot waves of 1954 seem very far away.   *Photo courtesy of Metro Conservation Authority*

and cried. We are getting $8,900 for our house. It's wonderful. We didn't expect it. We'll build our own house. I spray the house with creasol all the time.
Feb. 21.
We've got the flu again.
March 21.
The beginning of spring. The township haven't given us our final cheque because we told them we couldn't move until the end of June. Rev. Lewis is going to look into it. We've had two offers of places to stay in case we can't stay here. Roy is off for two weeks for the trapping. He came in at 1:30 with 13 rats. The prices average $1.60 a pelt, the best for years. Last year he got 60 cents to $1.

The police came to the door and told us we had to vacate at a moment's notice. We went to June's place and stayed there until the danger was over.
March 22.
We were warned again today by the police and tonight we were without lights for hours. The storm is bad. Winds high. Don't think we are in any danger. The river isn't too high.
March 23.
Today we got our final cheque for $3,382.10 and out of that we pay DVA $2,100.
March 31.
We went to see our land this afternoon. The roads were bad. It's 500 feet above Toronto and there's no water around.

The Patricks were still in their house as late as August 1955 and Mrs. Patrick found it frightening if she was there alone of an evening. Her health problems and the necessary heart surgery meant one delay after another. Almost two years passed before they were able to move into their new home. At that, she says she considers they were lucky.

CHAPTER THIRTEEN

DR. LORD AND FLOOD CONTROL

While Hurricane Hazel left a legacy of destruction never before equalled in Ontario, it did have some lasting, positive results. The Metropolitan Toronto and Region Conservation Authority, a vast, complex organization, internationally known and admired, is a creature of the flood, spawned out of the concern and resolve that never again would such an event catch the area unprepared.

Considering that Canada's first experiment in metropolitan government had only come into being in the spring of 1953, it is likely that without the impetus of Hurricane Hazel such a major amalgamation of conservation authorities, with all their natural local sensitivities, would not have occurred until much later. Hazel's heavy toll of eighty-one lives and $25 million worth of damage had a shock value that sent ripples of concern across all political boundaries.

It would be a mistake, however, to think there was no interest in conservation or flood control prior to Hazel. At least as far back as the 1930s there were a number of citizens' groups, notably the Ontario Conservation and Reforestation Association and the Federation of Ontario Naturalists, advocating various courses of action with regard to the environment. The year 1946 saw the passing of the Conservation Authorities Act by the Government of Ontario. The Act allowed the formation of a conservation authority where the local municipality sought government approval of such a move, and where the local citizens would agree to the responsibility of managing the authority. Costs would be shared by the province and municipality and each authority would have jurisdiction over a watershed, regardless of the number of municipalities it encountered.

What Hurricane Hazel did do was to act as a spur that galvanized governments and existing organizations into immediate co-operative action and long-range planning, the effects of which are still in evidence today.

Only four days after Hazel, the Meteorological Office on Bloor Street was the site of a meeting, "To Consider Ways and Means of Providing More Protection from Flood Damage".

A list of those in attendance at a second meeting eight days later attests to the wide-ranging concern that something must be done to prevent a repetition of the damage caused by Hazel. K. G. Higgs, Humber Valley Conservation Authority, Bolton; C. E. Bush, J. W. Murray, H. F. Crown, Conservation Branch, Department of Planning and Development; Dr. D. V. Anderson, Department of Lands and Forests, Maple; Eric Baker, Vice-Chairman, Humber Valley Conservation Authority; Donald Scott, Metropolitan Works Department; Andrew Thomson, Controller, Meteorological Division; P. D. McTaggart-Cowan, Assistant Controller, Meteorological Division; W. E. Turnbull, Officer-in-Charge, Dominion Public Weather Office, Malton; K. T. McLeod, Superintendent, Public Weather Meteorological Division; C. C. Boughner, Superintendent, Climatological Services, Meteorological Division.

At the time of the hurricane there were four conservation authorities: Etobicoke–Mimico, Humber, Don, and Rouge–Dufferin–Highland–Petticoat. While each had some measure of success, there was a real struggle for funds and it was becoming apparent that a more substantial financial basis would have to be established. Thus Hazel inadvertently gave birth to the Metropolitan Toronto and Region Conservation Authority, which at the time of its official inauguration in 1957 had twenty-three participating municipalities.

A. H. Richardson, Director of the province's Conservation Branch, headed the Authority that first year. The following year Dr. G. Ross Lord took over.

"It takes idealistic thinking to paint plans for any really worthwhile development involving two million people in a vitally expanding region," Dr. G. Ross Lord, P. Eng., Chairman of the Metropolitan Toronto and Region Conservation Authority, told an audience of conservationists several years later. A great deal of that imagination and planning was attributable to the enthusiastic engineer from Peterborough, who would be Chairman of the Authority from 1958 to 1972.

A man of intelligence and good humour, Dr. Lord was exactly the kind of man of dedication and purpose to become architect of flood control of such a vast area. He had received his training at the University of Toronto; had married his Peterborough hometown sweetheart, Nancy, whom he had known since she was fifteen years old. He'll tell you with a grin that once he saw her, he never let anyone else get near her. Together they returned to Toronto, and Lord took up a teaching position at his Alma Mater. He was to remain at the university as Professor of Engineering, and subsequently as head of the Department of Mechanical Engineering, until his retirement at the age of sixty-five in 1971.

The Ontario government had repeatedly sought his assistance on projects over the years, until he had become recognized as Canada's foremost hydraulic and flood-control engineer. In short, he was the logical choice to shepherd the infant Authority through its challenging early years of development. Anyone of lesser experience might have been daunted by the magnitude of the task ahead.

With 1,339 square miles (968 square miles, land-based, and 371 square miles, water-based), comprising all the watersheds of all streams entering Lake Ontario from Etobicoke Creek to Carruthers Creek and the shores of Lake Ontario within the boundaries of Pickering, Ajax, and Metro Toronto, all within its jurisdiction, the Authority had an enormous responsibility. Long-term planning for flood control was at the core of the Authority's mandate. But the moment flood control was considered, other allied concerns entered the picture: reforestation, recreation, fish and wildlife conservation, and stream-bank erosion.

At the time Dr. Lord became chairman of the Authority, he and a well-qualified team already had the beginnings of a comprehensive flood-control plan, which detailed construction of reservoirs, weirs, channel improvements, and floodplain regulations. The task ahead for him was to establish a long-term commitment to flood control with its constant, on-going planning and construction, coupled with environmental, recreational, and educational concerns, in a thousand-square-mile area of the most heavily populated part of Ontario. Within a decade the Clairville Dam and Reservoir had been brought into operation, thousands of acres of floodplain and valley lands had been acquired, flood-control channels had been constructed, and a modern flood-warning system established.

No one who lived through Hazel would need to be convinced of the value of a flood-warning system. The arrangement evolved by the Conservation Authority consists of a combination of technical measuring devices and information from voluntary rainfall observers. Recording stream gauges have been established on all the major rivers and tributaries within the Authority's boundaries and the system operates under the technical direction of the hydrometeorologist of the Conservation Authorities Branch, Ministry of Natural Resources. If these gauges begin to show an alarming rise in water level, it is the responsibility of the Authority to maintain contact with member municipalities and to advise all the appropriate people, including police, emergency services, and work departments, of the changing conditions.

Succeeding years saw the construction of another major flood-control dam, the G. Ross Lord Dam, and two smaller ones, Milne and Stouffville. Two important flood-control channels were also built, one through the village of Malton, the other on the west branch of the Don River at Bathurst Street and Sheppard Avenue.

The flood-control and water-management program brought with it ancillary benefits that are extremely well known. The Authority's conservation areas have provided beautiful recreational settings for the public to enjoy. Heart Lake, Boyd and Albion Hills, Glen Haffy, Black Creek, Claremont, and Cold Creek have all attracted people by the thousands, and are among the most popular recreational parkland areas in the country.

As happens to any vital, growing organization, the Authority developed into a multi-faceted organization. A tree and shrub nursery was established at the Boyd Conservation Area. A fish hatchery was constructed at Glen Haffy. A special outdoor school became part of the Albion Hills Conservation Field Centre. Black Creek Pioneer Village was adopted as a pioneer program, and is used as an educational project to demonstrate the importance of renewable natural resources in the lives of our forefathers.

Of the 25,000 acres of land under Authority jurisdiction at the beginning of 1977, more than 7,800 were in conservation areas, which attract a million and a half visitors annually. Fourteen areas offer boating, fishing, hiking, camping, skiing, swimming, rifle-range and trap shooting, archery, wildlife study, and maple-syrup making. It would be impossible to measure the impact the Authority has on many thousands of lives through the education programs for students, teachers, and the general public.

One of the most recent developments of the Authority is the Kortright Centre for Conservation, so named to honour the late Dr. Frank Kortright, one of Canada's foremost conservationists. He was the man responsible for originating the Sportsmen's Show, which over the years has raised $9 million for conservation. He was a man of extraordinary dedication to the cause of environmental concerns for our renewable resources, long before that became a public theme.

By 1978, thirty-five of thirty-seven erosion-control and bank-stabilization projects in hand had been completed. Topographic mapping of rivers had been completed, and planning for flood emergencies was in the process of being reviewed with each regional municipality.

Yet twenty-five years after Hazel, Dr. Lord says only about forty per cent of the original flood-control masterplan has been implemented. The reasons are not difficult to understand. From the outset there had been the need to purchase thousands of acres of river valleys and potential floodplains. Once regulations had been passed prohibiting dwellings on flood-vulnerable lands, the only fair approach to private owners was to buy their properties, make them part of the Authority lands, and remove forever the possibility of another Raymore Drive tragedy. As a result of this policy the Authority now owns more than 26,000 acres in and around Metro. With the full effects of inflation, however, the property-acquisition program can now cost between $1,000 and $2,000 an acre.

The accomplishments and achievements of the Authority are due not only to the co-operation and goodwill of governments, provincial and municipal, but in even greater measure to men like Dr. G. Ross Lord, who, after fifteen years as Chairman, remained another eight years as provincial representative. And the Authority owes a great debt of gratitude to the volunteer members whose diligence and creativity have made the achievements possible, as well as to members of the Metropolitan Toronto and Region Conservation Foundation, who have sought out financial aid.

Of all the work accomplished over the past quarter-century, none bears greater testimony to the value of the Authority than the present-day look of the Humber Valley. Where Hurricane Hazel ripped through, leaving a tangled, unspeakable mess, there is today an idyllic park, one of the most picturesque and beautiful in the entire province. It is enjoyed by thousands of people, summer and winter, but appreciated most by those who have watched the almost miraculous transformation effected by the Metropolitan Parks Department since 1954.

THE FUTURE - WHAT IF....?

A quarter of a century after Hazel, Toronto is a city on the threshold of the 1980s, a vibrant, living city that attracts most of the immigrants coming to Canada. It's a place coming of age and beginning to be comfortable with itself, beginning to accept itself without the constant sheepish comparison with other places. It can look at its physical make-up, enjoy its big-city feel, and still treasure its village-like neighbourhoods. It can laugh at some of its very prim and proper past and joke about some of its solid citizenry, while still appreciating their underlying values. It's a city that is growing up and doing it well.

The skyline that was once dominated by the Royal York Hotel is now ornamented by dozens of towers and skyscrapers, the golden geometrics of the Royal Bank, the dominant white column of the Bank of Montreal, and the silver needle of the CN Tower among them.

In the 1960s and 1970s, the city has rocked with the counterculture, the drug culture, and Rochdale; has watched the giant O'Keefe Centre come into being; and has seen Ed Mirvish rescue the Royal Alexandra and turn it into a dazzling jewel. The curving shapes of the prize-winning City Hall have become so familiar that they now draw comments only from visitors or newcomers, and Henry Moore's sculpture "The Archer" no longer attracts the arrows of the Philistines.

Expansion, growth, and development have been monumental in the last twenty-five years. With a new Massey Hall, the addition already made to the Art Gallery of Ontario, and the Royal Ontario Museum closed for a complete revamping and enlarging, Toronto's cultural institutions will rank, in size at least, with those of the world's great cities.

And there are institutions on the scene that owe their existence to no buildings. Toronto has authors like Robertson Davies and Morley Callaghan; musicians like Glenn Gould. We have media thinkers like Marshall McLuhan; politicians like Bill Davis; and a government that goes back to the early 1940s: the Honourable Pauline McGibbon, the first woman lieutenant-governor, who has set a precedent for superb performance that will be nearly impossible to match; Dr. Morton Shulman of iconoclastic fame; television stars like Lloyd Robertson and Harvey Kirck, and the unflappable Fred Davis. Not to mention Gordon Sinclair, King of Broadcasters, the same age as the century itself, defying all imitators with his instinctive change of pace from bombastic to bountiful, tenacious to temperate. His comments can light up CFRB's switchboard like a Christmas tree any day he chooses.

And then, as an indisputable institution, there is the ubiquitous Pierre Berton, a Canadian colossus with a conscience and a clutch of careers in the newspaper, magazine, radio, television, and publishing fields, each one more successful than the last.

Yorkville, the hippie haven of the 1960s, has undergone a metamorphosis that has spawned the Hazelton Lanes look of the 1970s. And downtown, the new Eaton

Centre, with its vaulted domes of glass and chrome, contrasts with the heritage-preserved lines of a spankingly refurbished Simpson's, officially designated an historic landmark. Oddly, for a city that is one of the continent's leading production centres of English-language television, the grand old lady CBC still struggles along in a tangled jungle of thirty-odd buildings that is a nightmare to artists, production people, and cost accountants alike. That did not hinder the emergence in the 1960s and 1970s of artists and creative people who not only made it at home, but garnered appreciation elsewhere: Maureen Forrester, Lois Marshall, Gordon Lightfoot, Neil Young, Anne Murray, Kate Reid, Margaret Atwood, Karen Kain, and many others.

The city has opened its doors to draft dodgers from the United States and the Vietnam War, immigrants from a hundred countries, and refugees from a dozen wars, including most recently the "boat people" fleeing Southeast Asia, until today a subway-car ride is like a journey in the company of a miniature United Nations. The newcomers have brought with them their languages and cultures, and made it possible for Torontonians to dine out every night of the week on a different cuisine. It is to be hoped the future will hold a greater exchange than dinner menus.

Every decade is a decade of change. There is nothing new in that. What was new about the 1960s and 1970s was the rate of that change, our attitudes towards the changes and towards ourselves. The sexual revolution and the women's liberation movement, coupled with a sophisticated world of technology that touched on every phase of our lives, have turned us suddenly from the ingenuous innocence of the booming 1950s, through the euphorically hopeful 1960s, to the complicated, sometimes convoluted world of complexity of 1979. In what other era would a Prime Minister Trudeau and a Margaret Trudeau belong?

It is not an age or an era that finds Toronto any longer disbelieving of catastrophe. The feeling that nothing bad could happen to us vanished along with the hoola hoop and crinolines under skirts. We have become a more mature city and we know our vulnerabilities.

Impenetrable traffic tie-ups in even the slightest rain make us well aware of our weather problems. That question of mobility in a sprawling city of millions of cars as well as people is a vital one. In a time of crisis it could be of paramount importance.

Could a disaster like Hurricane Hazel happen again? A good man to ask is Dr. Patrick Duncan McTaggart-Cowan, Director of Canada's Meteorological Service in the late 1950s and mid-1960s. He built Simon Fraser University in the late 1960s, and became its first President and then went on to head the Science Council of Canada. Hurricane Hazel has not been his only brush with disaster; he headed the task force Operation Oil in the wake of the *Arrow* oil spill in Nova Scotia in the early 1970s.

Dr. McTaggart-Cowan thinks there is no doubt it *could* happen again; but he does not believe there would be the same toll of lives. He recalls that the forecast predicting Hazel's arrival was dead on; the trouble was that too few people believed it. Predicting a hurricane in Toronto was like predicting a three-foot fall of snow on July 10. No one would take you seriously.

He recounts how Fred Turnbull took a call from a TTC Disaster Manager. The call came in when the eye of the hurricane was over Thornhill and Mississauga, and since all was quiet, the TTC man wondered if he should let all his people go home. Turnbull advised him to wait twenty minutes and the storm would be back from a different direction. Dr. McTaggart-Cowan cites the instance as the perfect example of how very little people knew of the nature of a hurricane.

The Meteorological Service of Canada, then under the Department of Transport, subsequently became the Atmospheric Environment Service, a part of the newly formed Department of the Environment. (In the 1970s even the names of things became more complicated.)

The Hazel experience was responsible for one major change. Afterwards, the meteorological people did try to get much closer to the media in talking about very unusual events. According to Dr. McTaggart-Cowan, that was where things went awry. "Had the media really picked up the forecast, picked up the story, flogged it twenty-four hours in advance, people might have been sensitized. But it was 1954; people weren't as glued to the radios as they were during the war. It was the time between the war and the sixties, that lull. Today the media would get right on it."

If a hurricane were to strike again, a number of parks would be devastated, but Dr. McTaggart-Cowan feels we have done a pretty good job of building bridges and dams and clearing floodplains as a place of residence for anyone. By contrast, certain other areas give cause for concern, like the Gatineau River near Ottawa, where people regularly have to evacuate their homes during spring flooding. So there are still homes built on floodplain lands. He is convinced people today are much more prone to respond to warnings to leave property because of danger, from whatever source, and cites the Three Mile Island example in Pennsylvania, where a nuclear leak caused concern and a mass exodus. Very few people refused to move, in marked contrast to the events during Hurricane Hazel.

He does sound a note of caution though, saying democracy has a way of going back to sleep. He is far more sanguine about the steps taken after Hazel than about the steps "taken by the Feds after the *Arrow* oil spill". After Hazel, governments were quick and responsive; there was a political will to do the job. "After the *Arrow* oil spill," he says sadly, "there was no real political will to do it."

Climatologist Bev Cudbird and conservationist Dr. G. Ross Lord share Dr. McTaggart-Cowan's view about the possibilities of another hurricane. The climatologist, who deals with statistical data about weather patterns, talks not only of possibility, but of very definite probability. Statistically, a storm like Hazel has a return period of thirty years. That means, according to statistical patterns, a storm like Hazel, or a storm which brings precipitation of more than five inches of rain within twenty-four hours, is likely to occur again within thirty years. The year 1979 marks the twenty-fifth anniversary of Hazel, as we know.

The way in which people, individually and collectively, deal with emergencies and the possibilities of emergency is remarkable. How many sensible, intelligent, mature adults take even the basic precautions against mundane home emergencies? The Canadian Safety Council suggests that an average home should be equipped with a first-aid kit, smoke detectors, and a small fire extinguisher. The householders should know how to use the equipment and when; should have emergency phone numbers readily visible; and should have a planned escape route from the house which every member of the family knows and understands. The Safety Council repeats this message regularly, and at times must find the results disheartening; no doubt the readers of this book are above reproach – or perhaps like everyone else, full of good intentions to get that smoke detector installed, and so on.

It is, then, not too surprising that Metropolitan Toronto, home of 2.25 million people, should finally, in
1979, find itself with a fully documented emergency plan.
For a number of years the provincial and federal governments held the reins on any overall approach to emergencies. But in 1975 they decided to vacate the role of
emergency planners, and the responsibility was passed to
the municipalities.

Metro Council decided that the Metro police force
should become the co-ordinating body and Police Chief
Harold Adamson would have that responsibility added to
his normal duties. As of January 1, 1976, the Metro police took over and Chief Adamson inherited people,
emergency equipment, a few buildings, and a hodge-
podge of plans. Then the job of trying to create some order out of chaos began. One old police station was relin-
quished, another kept. An installation at Aurora, constructed as a reserve site of operations for Metro officials
in case of a nuclear attack, has been retained.

Because of the layered structure of Metro itself, Chief
Adamson set to work with a Metropolitan Emergency
Measures Advisory Planning Board. With representa-
tives from a score of agencies, as well as police forces and
fire departments, the major strategy of co-ordination was
begun. When Hurricane Hazel struck in 1954, there were
thirteen police forces and just as many fire departments,
and no co-ordinating body whatsoever. The bridges that
proved so vulnerable were mostly old, dating from before
the First World War.

It has taken two and a half years and several hundred
meetings to arrive at the publication of the *Metropolitan
Toronto Police Emergency Planning Guide*. This is a manual
that spells out the structure, role, and chain of communication for emergencies for the Metro police and the many
organizations that range from ambulance and social serv-

ices, Hydro, Bell, and TTC, to Consumers' Gas. Though there is an obvious need for one group to be the co-ordinating body, this new structure, which will have the backing and authorization of special by-laws, has already caused some critical comment and mutterings about dictatorial powers of the police.

For Police Chief Adamson and Colonel John Hailey Pollard, Co-ordinator of Emergency Planning, there is the concern that people almost always plan for the emergency of yesterday. But the crisis of today and tomorrow may be very different. They are convinced that they could cope with another Hurricane Hazel, thanks to sophisticated communications which would allow the deployment of rescue teams and proper warnings to people at hazard; better roads and bridges than existed before; and a media-alert population that could be kept well informed by radio and television.

The emergency plans just now evolved are concerned with additional crises that belong more particularly to 1979; nuclear hazards top the list, but there are other potential hazards: shipments of chlorine or other dangerous chemicals crashing and leaking, for example; airplane crashes; debris from space hitting part of the city; and so on.

Chief Adamson, while confident about the emergency procedures now in place, admits that there are some emergencies for which you just cannot prepare, such as earthquakes and the possibilities of nuclear disasters. Evacuation of a major centre like Toronto, he feels, would be almost impossible; he has always to be conscious of the ingredient of panic. Awareness of that danger is implicit in the ways in which information would be worded through the media in event of any emergency. Today there is also a genuine awareness of the need for information, and in any incident, a communications centre will be established at once; Chief Adamson recalled how this had been done in a hostage-taking in Toronto within recent years.

The public will be made aware of much of the emergency planning, and all agencies involved in the plan – from St. John's Ambulance to the Red Cross and a variety of other social services – will probably find the manual the emergency Bible. There is nothing secret about the voluminous document, with the possible exception of those parts which deal with the apprehension of criminals, which it would be foolhardy to publicize.

Like Chief Adamson, Colonel Pollard, Co-ordinator of Emergency Planning, is accustomed to thinking and dealing with crisis. Previously Commissioner of Emergency Services, he has had the opportunity to visit NORAD and to study the surveillance system that exists there. He is aware that while we are doing a lot of talking about reactors, as a result of the Pennsylvania nuclear leak and the Ontario incidents, these are problems of radiation only. It is incredible to him that people have become conditioned to the enormous number of silos along our border that hold projectiles that "would make anything that could happen at Pickering look penny ante". He does express concern, however, about the Pickering site lying immediately adjacent to the biggest population centre in Canada. He speaks seriously about the SALT talks and believes that we have become anaesthetized to the risks of nuclear disasters that are not accidental.

Much of the emergency planning discussed here has come into being because of the disaster of Hurricane Hazel. Twenty-five years later there is a considerable legacy that is positive: the excellent work of the conservation authority; a new awareness of a region's vulnerabilities in time of crisis; and attempts to organize the communities' resources to meet emergencies.

This fall, the Humber Valley, a blaze of autumn colour, is a picturesque and lovely setting for family picnics, evening campfires, and exciting fishing for salmon. The river valley from Dundas south past the Old Mill and the charming stone bridge is now one of the best-used and best-loved parks in the city. It echoes to the nostalgic sound of voices across water and the cries of gulls, terns, and Canada geese. Many of those who enjoy its winding paths and clear running stream may think it has always been like this. But there is, in that valley, a giant boulder of red granite, and on it a bronze plaque with the names of five firemen. And there are those who remember.

CHAPTER FIFTEEN

THREE STORIES

The story of Hurricane Hazel is the story of people, the people who lived through it and remember the experience. It is fitting that the final chapter of this book should be devoted to the stories of people who suffered at the hands of the hurricane. First, the story of Pat and Bud Irwin, who lived on Fairglen Crescent beside the Humber.

For them, the weekend began as something special. On Thursday they celebrated their fifth wedding anniversary. Bud's gift of five perfect red roses, carefully arranged in their best vase, graced their livingroom. Friday night, when they went shopping, they proudly mailed a cheque that marked the halfway term of their mortgage, and they had a brand-new washing machine installed in their basement.

Because it was such a miserable night, they had offered to shop for a pregnant neighbour and had returned to the neighbour's house and visited there until 10:30 p.m. When they were about to leave for their own house across the street, they found six to eight inches of water on the street, and had to borrow rubber boots.

At home, their first concern was for the new washing

machine in the event of water in the basement. Pat Irwin then became alarmed about the amount of water that was rising swiftly and began "phoning for help . . . fire departments, police departments, requesting that somebody come quickly with boats." She remembers her calls being met with a very casual air, and finally, in mounting fright, calling the *Telegram*, where she was just told by some voice that she had the wrong department. She recalls that she became very upset and yelled that somebody had better listen to her and get some boats to Fairglen Crescent or people were going to die.

The Irwins heard a loud crash from their basement and discovered that a log had been driven right through a basement window, and water was now rushing in. Thoroughly frightened, they dashed back upstairs and out their front door, hoping to drive away in their car. The water outside the house was now so swift and deep that Bud lost his footing. He clutched Pat's hand to right himself, and somehow the two of them fought their way back and regained the height of the front porch.

There they found that the house door was locked and they didn't have a key. In one of those illogical moments in a crisis, they stood arguing about whether or not they should break the front window to regain entry to the house. Pat recalls warning what a new window would do to their careful budget.

The window was just the first of many things to go that night. In a very short time, the lower part of the house was filled with water and Pat and Bud sought the safety of the second storey of their home. Even then, Pat recalls, there was the crazy contradiction of acting normally under circumstances that were anything but normal. She brought the vase of roses upstairs. She remembers asking Bud what he was thinking of, dropping his soaking wet clothes on top of their satin bedspread. Although she did not stop to reason things out, Pat insisted on getting out most of their sheets and tying them together. When Bud didn't see much sense to that, she remembers cajoling him into it by saying she was the one who would have to do the laundry.

Then began a terrifying watch. From their second-storey window, the Irwins saw their car drift slowly back out their driveway, "almost as if an invisible person were driving it", turn in the current, and be carried away out of sight.

A pounding, bumping sound from underneath them worried and puzzled them. It proved to be their piano, an inherited luxury, floating so high in the water on the ground floor that it was bouncing and hitting the ceiling. The entire ground floor of the house was filled with floodwater.

Rescue boats were now in operation. The Irwins watched from their window as some people were saved and others were swept to their deaths. Because their house was two-storey, and looked perhaps more durable, rescuers headed first for the most critical and for those in the most immediate danger. From their window perch the Irwins could see one neighbour spread-eagled against a gabled section of roof, and called repeatedly to him to hold on. Their calls to the men in boats to come for that man for some reason were unheeded, or unheard, or perhaps the man was hidden by an angle of the roof. They watched in horror as that part of the flood-ravaged house floated away into the blackness.

Suddenly their own house began to move. Slowly at first, and then with gathering momentum. Pat Irwin tearfully remembers praying that if this was to be the end, her husband's life would be spared. "To this day, I don't know if I just loved Bud so much I wanted him to live . . . or if I felt there was no way I could face life without him. So I don't know if I was being selfish or un-selfish."

The Irwins' house travelled downstream three hundred yards, caught on something, held. Outside, the water was up to the window, where they stood clinging to the centre part of the frame. There were agonizing moments, waiting, wondering if the house would remain stationary, or be swept away again on the current. A rescue boat was attempting to reach them, but was having great difficulty in the current. In a tight voice of desperation, Pat called out, "Make a good catch," and threw the tied-together sheets out into the wind. P.C. Jim Crawford and Herb Jones were able to catch the sheets. Pulling steadily on them, they were able to draw alongside the Irwins and take them to safety. The Irwins stepped from their second-storey window right into the rowboat.

Next day there was still such disbelief about what had happened that Mrs. Irwin's relatives tried to comfort her by saying they would go back and help her clean out her house and get things back into order; obviously, they believed she was hysterically exaggerating what had happened. They were stunned to find the place where the house had stood empty, and the house itself way downstream.

One of the few items retrieved from the water-filled house was the vase of red roses, which somehow remained intact. That was the first time Mrs. Irwin broke down. The next bitter blow was to see her home break into pieces and disintegrate. For years after there were nightmares of the water rising and a house being torn from its foundations.

Next, John M. Hunter's story. John Hunter was a teacher at the Island public school in Toronto who, after a visit to his girlfriend's house, left at 10:30 p.m. to drive home to Thistletown, joking that he had a date with Hazel, and had to go.

"The first part of the trip to Thistletown was relatively uneventful. It was windy but the rain had stopped. However, as I drove up Albion Road past the Elms and Summerlea (now Humber Valley) Golf Course I saw a car I thought was making a turn. However, as I swerved to the other lane to pass, I discovered that the car was not turning but rather had stopped because of water flowing across the road. I took my foot off the gas momentarily and hit the brakes. They were wetted out. By the time I got my foot back on the gas the engine was coughing. Then it died and the car rolled to a stop at the side of the road.

"This was my first car, just bought the previous spring and over the summer. I had spent a number of nights sleeping on the front seat. I decided that this would just be another of these. I sat in my car about one hundred yards from the Humber bridge.

"After my car stopped, two cars went by me. The first, a Cadillac, steamed right through, over the bridge and up the hill. The second, a Pontiac, slowed to ask if I was okay. I told them I was fine and to keep going or they would stall. I was too late. Their car stalled just a few feet up the road. Their concern for their fellow human beings had them in the same predicament I was in.

"I curled up on the front seat but soon heard the water rushing across the floor. It was getting deeper!

"Then the car moved. It was slowly turned by the current so that it slid off the road with its nose into the current. Once the water crossed the road it became much deeper. The car became nearly full. I had to get out.

"The only way I could do this was to force my body between the door and door jamb, literally forcing the door open against the current. I managed to get out of the car but found myself standing beside my car, in freezing cold water up to my armpits, with one hand holding the door handle and the other holding the side-view mirror.

"I felt the two men in the other stalled car were much better off than I was. Their car had not shifted as mine had, but rather had turned over, first onto its side and then onto the roof. Its occupants were sitting on the top smoking. I could see the glow of their cigarettes, and remember thinking how lucky they were.

"My most pressing problem now seemed to be to get out of the water, which was so cold that my legs were going numb. Just as I pulled myself up on the roof I heard a crash, some calls for help, then nothing. The other car had turned over, throwing its two passengers into what was now white water. The dam had gone out in Woodbridge and the Albion Road was like the rapids of the Niagara River. They drowned.

"It was at this point that I knew I was going to die. I sat on the roof of the car, alone in the darkness for what seemed like a lifetime.

"After about two hours the Thistletown volunteer fire department arrived on the scene. When their searchlight came on it offered some hope of rescue. Their first attempt was to wade out on the road to reach me. The current was too fast and they washed off the road. They then took the ladders off their truck and tied them from tree to tree on the far side of the road, making a bridge which ended directly in front of me. Then they floated me a rope. I had little problem getting it, and using my best Scout training fastening it around my waist in a bowline. I was saved!

"I waved to the firemen and they started the winch on their truck. The rope pulled me out into the rushing waters on the road. Halfway across the road I felt a snap.

I turned over in the water and was swept past my car while I frantically groped for something to hang on to.

"The rope was broken – it was swim or drown, and when you are twenty-one years old you sure don't want things to end. I swam. A large object hit me in the back, leaving a bruise the size of a football. I swam towing twenty or thirty feet of thick rope. I swam over three fences and was lucky enough that the rope didn't tangle in them.

"While I swam two firemen ran along the edge of the water keeping a light on me. When I came out they helped me to a house near by, where the people were extremely kind. After staying the rest of the night they lent me clothes and footwear to go back into the city. Two policemen gave me carfare. Everyone helped.

"The next day my father, who was the bank manager in Thistletown, walked down the hill to see the flood damage. He saw a car that looked like mine – up to its windows in water. He didn't know until later, when phone service was restored, that it was mine. The car was a total wreck, but the insurance money bought an engagement ring – and that's another story."

For another survivor, Danny Ukrainetz, there were no happy memories associated with Hurricane Hazel. With some stories it is best to let the storyteller use his own words, without comment. What follows is such a story:

"Four close friends decided to go fishing to Long Point on Lake Erie early in the morning of October 15th. We all got our fishing gear and took off for Long Point. We, meaning my brother Walter, close friends Ben and John. My name is Danny.

"We got to Long Point very early to make sure we were in for good fishing for bass, as the season opened at midnight that day.

"John and Ben had bought a three-horsepower motor outboard and were eager to see if it was worth the money they had invested in it, which was very cheap. Being the most mechanical in mind, I was appointed to be the motor operator by the three members.

"We rented a wooden boat from the local marina. The boat was in fair shape, had two oars, one anchor, and four lifejackets, which consisted of two square cushions tied together with two strings. They were old and very well used for the purpose to sit on in the boat while fishing. We were all set to go fishing. I drove while the boys checked their lines and rods.

"When we finally decided our fishing spot, off we casted and then began the eager task. Who and where would the first fish be caught? There were a few small bets. The time was about 6:30 a.m.

"We proceeded to change spots within a hundred yards. But no one of us even got a bite, as the day passed very warm and sunny. About 2:00 p.m. we had seen several boats coming from across the bay with a very high shore called 'Turkey Point'. Each boat that went by us showed us a string of fish that made our eyes bulge. So we decided to go across to Turkey Point and get the big ones.

"Across was approximately five miles. We did go. We soon were involved in some very good fishing. At one time Ben had two fish on his line at the same time. We soon had our limit of fish at approximately 6:45, when we noticed that the time was late and we would be late for homecoming, as all four of us were married. We also noticed that there were no other boats fishing. The sun was still shining. The water was as calm as glass.

"We started to pack our gear and start our slow putt putt back towards Long Point.

"John, as part owner of the motor, wanted to drive the boat home. He did. We were still delighted with our catch of fish. John was the navigator, hitting for Long Point.

"As we were leaving Turkey Point the banks are very high there. I suddenly looked up and could see this very dark cloud coming behind us. I did say to the boys, 'Gee, that's a dark cloud, maybe we should turn back.' But the boys joked and said, 'The wind is behind us. That will help us get there faster.' The wind had just started to pick up. We joked and laughed while John was full speed towards Long Point.

"Very shortly the waves started and the wind was getting stronger. I looked at the time and it was 7:00 p.m. I then said to the boys I think we should put our lifejackets on. We did. Brother Walter had quite a time with his jacket, not knowing that the long string was to be tied between his legs and back to the cushion in back. By then the wind and waves were so high that we started to get some water splashing into the boat from the back.

"Seconds later it got dark. The rain and wind so bad that all of us were scared. The waves got so big they soon filled the boat. The motor had already been stopped. I proceeded to give orders to hang on to the wooden boat. We arranged ourselves so we could balance our bodies with the wooden boat. Brother Walter took the very front or bow. Ben got the back and got a hold of the motor. John and myself got on each side, with all our bodies dangling in the water. The wind and rain were so strong we could hardly see each other. It got worse. At one time I could barely see, but the boat was bobbing so high that I saw my brother Walter clear out of the water, hanging onto the bow of the boat.

"John and myself grasped our hands across the boat, which by now had turned bottom side up. The boat seemed to start rolling over top of me. John and me let go of our hand lock and I went under water. When I came up I could see the boat and the boys bobbing about twenty feet behind me. I could in no way get back to the boat. Instead I was bounced further away. Panic hit me. I could not see them, but could hear them calling, 'Help! Help!'

"The bay was just one grey mess of water. The waves were not even, just waves crossing in every direction. Again I panic. I went down then up gasping and swallowed some water. I am not a very good swimmer, but could dive. I thought to try to get my shoes off. They were laced too tight. The lifejacket seemed to be too heavy. The car keys are in my pocket. How will the boys get home, because I will never make it. My mind raced through most of my life. My wife. My daughters just eight and ten. My wallet is wet. How long before they find me? I think I'm out in the Atlantic by now. The waves were so fast and hard it felt like someone was slapping the back of my head with a wet mop.

"I soon got exhausted. If I saw a wave I dove under only to come up and get belted with another. It seemed to me like forever. Some time later I saw a boat and called 'Help! Help!' at the top of my lungs. The boat was soon out of sight. That was it. That was my last hope. Wind, rain, and hail not letting up the least bit.

"I don't know how long it took but I saw the boat again. 'Help! Help!' They saw me. They were coming to save me. I got more strength in me than ever. They were beside me. I saw one man throw a round lifesaver to me and the rope followed. I made one grab and had it. Locked my arms around it, exhausted. Now fellows, it's all up to you. I will never let go.

"The rope too slack. Is it broke? And then the boat was on top of my back. God I will get caught in the prop of the motor. I'm still gripping the lifesaver, thinking if I go the lifesaver goes with me. Then a tug and I come to the surface. That was the most beautiful feeling I've ever had. Pull, pull boys, I will never let go. When they pulled me even, there were my brother Walter and Ben pulling and other mates helping. I found I was so stiff I could not lift my legs over the rail of the boat.

"We hugged and cried. Then came the blow. Where is John? Walter thought he was with me.

"The Captain of the boat was Department of Lands and Forests and he said, 'He's got to be in this area somewhere.' We looked back and forth till after 11:30. We did not find John.

"We went to shore and there were quite a number of people there and the Simcoe OPP. Some lady took us three into a warm room and gave us some hot coffee and cookies and made us comfortable. The OPP came in and asked a few questions about John, how well we knew him. We were all very close. Same church, same ball team, dancing. The OPP suggested it would be better if us boys would say the bad news to his wife. The three of us did not think it was such a good idea.

"But after a discussion with the OPP they explained it would be better if someone was there that she knew personally. Better than let a cop come in the house and say your husband is missing, we have not found his body so we don't know if . . . or if . . . , then bye now, I am sorry, and politely leave.

"Well the burden was ours. I don't know how we made it to Hamilton. We spoke very little. Got lost three or four times. There were trees and wires all the way to Hamilton.

"We got to John's home at 3:00 a.m. That was a sad part. His wife, with a four-month-old baby, lived with her parents. She did come to the door and after we three walked into the house she broke in a loud cry. 'It's John. It's John. What happened?'

"We then tried to comfort her as much as possible saying that we are not sure John was gone. That he might have got blown adrift like me, away from the boat, and could be on some shore making his way home now. I don't think she took in all that. We left the house with her voice calling, 'John. John.'

"Early next morning Walter, Ben, John's father-in-law, and myself took off for Long Point. We got there about 7:30. The Simcoe police were waiting for us. We got in the police patrol boat to see if we could find John. There was no wind. It was very warm and the fishing boats were filling the bay with fishermen.

"As we approached one area fishermen waved us down and we complied. They had found John's body, floating upright with his hands up even with his shoulders. Myself and two OPP's pulled John out onto the boat deck. That is one sight I will never forget.

"A year later my brother Walter, his wife Mary, son George, and daughter Anna got killed in Stoney Creek by a CN train.

"So now is only Ben and myself left with that horrible experience of Hurricane Hazel."